Praise My Soul

Meditating
on
Hymns

Other Church Publishing Books by Nancy Roth

We Sing of God: a Hymnal for Children
Robert N. Roth and Nancy L. Roth, Editors
The Church Hymnal Corporation, 1989

Praying: a Book for Children
Nancy L. Roth
The Church Hymnal Corporation, 1991

A Closer Walk: Meditating on Hymns for Year A
Nancy Roth
Church Publishing Incorporated, 1998

Awake, My Soul! Meditating on Hymns for Year B
Nancy Roth
Church Publishing Incorporated, 1999

New Every Morning: Meditating on Hymns for Year C
Nancy Roth
Church Publishing Incorporated, 2000

Also:

An Invitation to Christian Yoga (Cowley, 2001)
The Breath of God: an Approach to Prayer (Cowley, 1990)
Organic Prayer (Cowley, 1993)
Meditations for Choir Members (Morehouse, 1999)

Praise My Soul

Meditating on Hymns

Nancy Roth

Church Publishing, New York

Library of Congress Cataloging-in-Publication Data
Roth, Nancy, 1936-
Praise my soul : meditating on hymns / Nancy Roth.
p. cm.
ISBN: 0898693748 (pbk.)
1. Episcopal Church--Hymns--History and criticism.
2. Hymns--Devotional use. 3. Church year meditations.
4. Hymns, English--United States--History and criticism.
BV340 .R695 2001
264'.23--dc 21
2001047715

Church Publishing Incorporated
445 Fifth Avenue
New York NY 10016

www.churchpublishing.org

5 4 3 2 1

Acknowledgments

This project could not have been accomplished without the help of my husband Bob, who provided both editorial advice and moral support, and the facilities of the Oberlin College Library, in particular the resource materials of the Dictionary of American Hymnology and the help of its custodian Mary Louise VanDyke.

In memory of

Stella Roth

Table of Contents

Introduction

I am delighted that Church Publishing has chosen to make available in this larger-print format a selection of the hymn meditations I wrote for the three volumes *A Closer Walk*, *Awake, My Soul!*, and *New Every Morning*.

Exploring the church's rich tradition of hymnody has been an important part of my life over the last few years. I have found myself drawn in an extraordinary way into the stories of the poets, saints, martyrs, and quite ordinary people who wrote our hymn texts. The words of a hymn draw me into God's presence, creating a quiet space for reflection and contemplation. Often I find that the texts voice my own prayer, like an alternative prayer book.

As I travel around the country leading workshops and retreats based on my work, I have found that, for others as well, meditating on hymn texts is a way to integrate head and heart. I hope that you will also have the pleasure of discovering the rich heritage we have received from our brothers and sisters in the faith whose words are part of our prayer and our song.

HOW TO USE THIS BOOK

PERSONAL DEVOTION

In the subtitle of this book, "Meditating on Hymns," I have used the word "meditating" in the traditional sense of reflecting upon a theme rather than in the more contemporary sense of emptying the mind. I suggest a simple pattern:

1. Preparing. It is helpful to prepare both physically and spiritually: by settling down in a comfortable position (but not so comfortable you will fall asleep!), paying attention to your breathing, trying to clear your mind of the cares of the day, and quietly offering this time of prayer to God.

Then read the text over, either silently or aloud, from *The Hymnal 1982* or another hymnal.

2. Picturing. The first part of every meditation introduces you to the writers of the hymns, suggests scriptural allusions in the texts, and provides other background that will help the words come

alive. During this part of the meditation, you listen in your imagination to the voices that first sang the hymn. When did they live? What did they believe? What were their lives like? How did they understand Scripture?

3. Pondering. Pause before continuing on to this part of the meditation, by sitting in silence for a while and perhaps reading the text over again slowly. In this part of the meditation, you are listening to God speaking to you through the hymn. What might this hymn mean in terms of your life and your journey with God? Is there some way in which God might be calling you to respond in a specific way to the messages you hear through this text?

The reflections I have written are intended only to be a catalyst for your own thinking and praying, so give yourself time to think about the text on your own.

4. Gathering. In conclusion, "gather together" your meditation in any way you find most helpful, such as writing down your insights or concluding with your own prayer of gratitude to God for the guidance the hymn provides.

5. Singing or Listening. Although this book is primarily about the texts of the hymns, this does not mean that we think the music is superfluous. Indeed, what inspired this project is the fact that the music is often so compelling that we neglect to pay adequate attention to the texts. So, finally, you may wish to wed words and music by singing the hymn yourself, or listening to it on a tape or CD.

PRAYER GROUPS

The above pattern would be an ideal focus for a Prayer Group, whether it be in the setting of your church or in your neighborhood or retirement community.

PREACHING AND CHRISTIAN EDUCATION

This book is a useful resource for those responsible for liturgy or preaching. Texts can be used as a springboard for sermons, and hymns can be a refreshing way to teach about Scripture, the Creed, church history, and "all the saints" who have gone before us.

QUIET DAYS, RETREATS, AND WORKSHOPS

In leading programs, quiet days, and retreats focusing on hymns, I have found the pattern of "preparing, picturing, pondering, gathering, and singing," to be a useful pattern which engages many aspects of our personalities—our hearts, our spirits, our minds, and even our physical selves, as we sing (and occasionally even dance!) a hymn. A similar pattern can be used for intergenerational or children's programs, using the added resource material in *We Sing of God: a Hymnal for Children* (Church Publishing, 1989).

CONCLUSION

The poetry of our hymns draws us beyond doctrine to faith, helping us grow in relationship to the mystery of the Holy Trinity, both infinitely beyond us and intimately close to us. The hymns of almost two millennia are our companions in prayer, helping us to sing in our own hearts the praises of our God:

"So has the Church, in liturgy and song,
in faith and love, through centuries of wrong,
borne witness to the truth in every tongue,
Alleluia!" (Hymn 420, "When in our music God is glorified")

Hymn 61 and 62

"Sleepers, wake!" A voice astounds us

Philipp Nicolai (1556–1608)

Philipp Nicolai was a Lutheran pastor in Unna, Westphalia. The text of *Wachet auf* was written during the time of a plague which killed over 1,300 people in his region. There were often as many as thirty daily burials in the churchyard beside the parsonage, so it was no wonder that Nicolai's thoughts turned to the life to come. He began the practice of writing daily meditations "to leave behind me (if God should call me from this world) as the token of my peaceful, joyful, Christian departure, or (if God should spare me in health) to comfort other sufferers whom he should also visit with the pestilence. . . ." This collection of meditations, entitled *Freuden-Spiegel des ewigen Lebens (A Joyful Mirror of Eternal Life)* contained the text and tunes of what eventually became known as the "King" and "Queen" of chorales: *Wachet auf* ("Sleepers, wake!") and *Wie schön leuchtet der Morgenstern* ("How bright appears the Morning Star," Hymn 496, 497).

The principal biblical reference in the text of *Wachet auf* is to the parable in Mt. 25:1–13, in which

which Jesus tells the story of ten bridesmaids waiting for the arrival of the bridegroom. Palestinian custom dictated that the bridegroom fetch his bride, with her attendants, from her parents' home to his own. Five of the bridesmaids were wise and had brought extra oil for their lamps; five were foolish, and had not. When the bridegroom was delayed, they slept, only to be awakened at midnight with a shout that the bridegroom was about to arrive. (The sentinel's voice reminds us of Isa. 52:8: "Listen! Your sentinels lift up their voices, together they sing for joy; for in plain sight they see the return of the Lord to Zion.") By now, the lamps of the foolish maidens had gone out, and they had to leave to buy more oil. It was only the wise maidens, prepared with ample oil for their lamps, who joyfully accompanied the bridegroom into the wedding banquet.

The final stanza of the hymn evokes the world of the writer of the Book of Revelation, drawing on the images in chapter 19:6–9: "Hallelujah! For the Lord our God the Almighty reigns. Let us rejoice and exult and give him the glory, for the marriage of the Lamb has come, and his bride has made herself ready."

The translation of *Wachet auf* in *The Hymnal 1982* is by Carl P. Daw, Jr. The tune, written by Nicolai at the same time as the text, appears in two harmonizations: by Praetorius and by J.S.Bach, who used the chorale in his Cantata 140.

Once again, the swiftly turning year brings us to Advent, the beginning of the church's calendar. When I was a child in Sunday School, I was taught that Advent was about "the four last things": death, judgment, heaven, and hell. I imagine that "death, judgment, heaven, and hell" were what Pastor Philipp Nicolai was gazing at, as he looked out into his churchyard pitted with so many newly dug graves. He surely awoke, as he never had before, to his own mortality.

"Sleepers, wake!" Most of us are asleep, when it comes to a sense of our mortality. Rushing through our days, trying to meet our own goals and others' expectations, we have little time to think about the end of life. And when we do have to face it, we are ill prepared.

So the sentinels of Advent remind us "Sleepers, wake!" Be ready! For what? For "death, judgment, heaven, and hell"?

No, this Advent sentinel astounds us by calling us, instead, to a wedding feast! We are invited to bring our lamps to welcome the Bridegroom, to hasten through the dark streets towards the gates of pearl to greet him. We can even hear the eager footsteps in the bass line of Bach's harmonization of the chorale. The Bridegroom is Jesus Christ, the Lamb of God. The feast is attended by saints and angels, accompanied by harps and cymbals. The sight is beyond imagining, the sound beyond wondering. We are swept along with the other guests into the city of God.

Perhaps it is easier to face preparing for the end of our lives if we think of the end as a wedding feast rather than "death, judgment, heaven, and hell." But the sentinel call is equally urgent. Be ready! And prepare enough oil for your lamps.

How do we prepare? With what oil can we sustain our light? The spaciousness of the great chorale may give us a hint. If you were to breathe at the pace of the chorale, with an inhalation or an exhalation for each measure or whole note, it might remind you to stop hurrying through life mindlessly. If you were to let the great arc of the melody open your soul to the mystery of God, it might remind you to make one of your priorities in life your relationship in prayer with the Bridegroom whom you are called to greet.

For it is prayer that sustains our light. Prayer that is, above all, a breathing in of the life at the source of our being: God's life and love. And then breathing it out again: God's life and love, into the world.

Praying in preparation for a wedding feast. A good way to begin the year. A good way to prepare for Christmas. A good way to prepare for eternity.

Hymn 81

Lo, how a Rose e'er blooming

German, 15th cent., tr. Theodore Baker (1851–1934), Friedrich Layritz (1808–1859), Harriet Reynolds Krauth Spaeth (1845–1925)

The prophecy of Isa. 11:1, "There shall come forth a shoot from the stump of Jesse, and a branch shall grow out of his roots," found expression in hymnody as early as the eighth century. A Greek hymn by Cosmas the Melodist, as translated by John Mason Neale, begins "Rod of the Root of Jesse, Thou, Flower of Mary born."

The text of "Lo, how a Rose e'er blooming" is the translation of the German carol, *Es ist ein' Ros entsprungen*, and dates from the fifteenth century. The earliest source is a manuscript from St. Alban's Carthusian Monastery preserved in the municipal library of Trier. According to the owner's mark on the inside cover, the manuscript is a prayer book which once belonged to a certain Brother Conrad the Carthusian of Mainz.

Although the hymn seems to have been current at the time of Luther (1483–1546), it was first published in a Roman Catholic hymnal, *Alte Catholische Geistliche Kirchengeseng,* in Cologne (1599). The poem originally consisted of twenty-three stanzas which related the events of the Christmas story as found in Lk. 1 and 2 and Mt. 2, giving special emphasis to the role of Mary.

It is interesting to note that, although the hymn originally referred to Mary as the rose, reformers sought to change the emphasis of the hymn to refer to Jesus. The rose tree has historically been held in special regard throughout Germany, and is still widely understood as a symbol for Mary or Jesus.

The text is set to the German carol tune associated with the words from the beginning.

I like to think about roses in winter. On a cold day, I welcome the early garden catalogs, with their photographs of exquisite blossoms with beautiful names: "New Dawn", *"Souvenir de Philémon Cochet,"* "Shadow Dancer," "Golden Celebration," "Tropicana," "Peace."

I wonder if the writer of "Lo, how a rose e'er blooming" knew the story of the rose, so uncannily similar to Christian history. He would not have been picturing the modern tea rose, that ingenious creation of hybridizers over the last several centuries, but rather a hardier flower. As the noted English garden writer Hugh Johnson comments,

> The ancestry of roses may seem a laborious way of approaching a delectable subject. But if one is to make any sense out of the bewildering variety of flowers grouped under that name today the only place to start is with the wild roses whose sap, in a cocktail of inextricable complexity, runs in their veins.[1]

The well-known rose hybridizer David Austin suggests that the history of the rose predates human history by many thousands of years, beginning with a simple flower with five petals which grew across the continents of the Northern Hemisphere. The first garden roses were probably cultivated in the Middle East and then spread by way of ancient Greece and Rome. They were eventually grown all over Europe. It is thought that perhaps Crusaders of the twelfth and thirteenth centuries brought specimens home on their return from the Holy Land. They were cherished for their medicinal properties as well as their beauty, and were widely cultivated in medieval monasteries.[2]

In our garden, because I do not spray them, I can observe how roses are integral to the natural ecosystem. Whether I approve or not, they feed beetles and aphids, who in turn become food for ladybugs and birds. Their roots hold firm the soil from erosion. In the climbing red rose by the front door, a mother robin annually raises a family.

When I can bring myself to cut a blossom, the fragrance of the garden enters the house, and the rose becomes a source of sensuous delight. When I was a child, I used to believe that little people made their homes in their petals, because roses were by far the most beautiful things I could think of in the natural world.

This beautiful flower began as a simple wildflower, much like the young woman of Hebrew lineage who was greeted one day by an angel. The message of the Son she bore spread in the Middle East and then to ancient Greece and Rome. His gospel was eventually to spread all over Europe, and beyond, preserved in large part by those same monks who tended the roses in their cloister gardens. Especially since the time of the Reformation, this gospel has had its hybridizers as well: Christianity today can surely be described, like the rose, as "a cocktail of inextricable complexity."

Thinking about roses in winter, like thinking about Mary's gift to the dark world, heals the human spirit, yearning in midwinter for the beauties of the summer garden.

Hymn 102

Once in royal David's city

Sts. 1–2 and 4–6, Cecil Frances Alexander (1818–1895); st. 3, James Waring McCrady (b. 1938)

Cecil Frances Humphreys was born in County Wicklow, Ireland, in 1818; her father was a Royal Marine, landowner and government agent. She published two popular collections of hymns for children before her marriage, during which time she and her sister ran a school for deaf-mutes. The profits from her *Hymns for Little Children* were designated for the school. She was a well-educated churchwoman, keenly interested in the Oxford Movement, who attended daily services and devoted time to the unfortunate. In 1850 she married the Rev. William Alexander, one of the most brilliant men in the Irish church, who became Bishop of Derry and Raphoe and, after his wife's death, primate of all Ireland.

Cecil Frances Alexander was to write 400 hymns, most of them for children. Her children's hymns are characterized by the use of images to capture a child's imagination, followed by instruction couched in simple language expressing theological truths. This is one of several hymns written by Cecil F. Alexander for her Sunday school class during the time she was teaching her students the Apostles' Creed. It was later published in her *Hymns for Little Children* (London, 1848).

This hymn illustrates the third article of the Creed: "who was conceived by the Holy Ghost, born of the Virgin Mary." Like her other hymns written to help her young students remember the articles of faith ("All things bright and beautiful," written to illustrate "Maker of heaven and earth," and "There is a green hill far away," explaining "suffered under Pontius Pilate, was crucified, dead, and buried"), this one is cherished by children and adults alike.

The text in *The Hymnal 1982* has been revised from Mrs. Alexander's original poem, which depicts a vision of childhood that is distinctly Victorian. Susan S. Tamke writes that, in nineteenth-century children's hymns,

> . . .the child is shown very clearly the virtues which he must cultivate to gain a heavenly reward. Chief among these virtues are submissiveness and obedience. The child is also warned against the temptations of frivolity—he must strive for earnestness. In fact, the image of a perfect Christian child presented by children's hymns is that of a monastic; he is disciplined, he contemplates God continually, he rejects worldly pleasures and he mortifies himself for any transgression.[3]

Therefore, a new third stanza by James Waring McCrady, a linguist and musician, has replaced the following lines by Mrs. Alexander:

> And, through all his wondrous childhood,
> He would honor and obey
> Love, and watch the lowly maiden,
> In whose gentle arms he lay;
> Christian children all must be
> Mild, obedient, good as he.[4]

Because of the extremely high infant and childhood mortality rate of Mrs. Alexander's era, it is not surprising that she closed her hymn with the suggestion that after death, "Like stars his children crowned all in white shall wait around." Tamke writes, "Death is clearly the final goal which these Victorian children are taught to anticipate."[5] In this era of better health care for both young and old, it is appropriate that Alexander's final lines have been replaced, now emphasizing the presence of Christ revealed to all the faithful in heaven.

With its tune, written in 1849 by Dr. Henry Gauntlett, the hymn has become known the world over through the annual Christmas Eve broadcasts of the Service of Nine Lessons and Carols by the choir of King's College, Cambridge.

Every year, on the calendar square marked "Christmas Eve," my husband and I write an appointment: 10:00 A.M.—King's College Chapel. Early that day, we make sure that our radio is tuned to the local public radio station. Sometimes, as 10:00 nears, we even take our phone off the hook. We turn our radio on at least five minutes early. And finally it happens. Over the airwaves comes the disembodied clear voice of one little boy: "Once in royal David's city / stood a lowly cattle shed, / where a mother laid her baby / in a manger for his bed: / Mary was that mother mild, / Jesus Christ her little child."

We wait for that moment all year long. After many visits there, we know King's College Chapel well. On our first visit, we were so overwhelmed with the beauty of the music that we had to take shelter in a side chapel to weep afterwards. We can imagine the dance of the child's voice in the amazing fan vaulting, and the dim light of dusk barely illuminating the stained glass windows. We can see the chapel filled with worshipers; we also have stood in long queues to get into services there.

We can see the choir of lay clerks and boys, wearing their red cassocks and white cottas. And, on Christmas Eve, we can hear them.

What is it about the voice of a boy that is so heart-achingly beautiful? It can be explained, of course, in acoustical or musical terms—something to do with vibrations or overtones. But I think it has to do with more than that. It has to do with our knowledge that this is a sound that will not last; that, one day, this little boy's voice will change and he will be on the way to becoming a tenor or baritone. It has to do with the temporary nature of childhood, and of life itself. The transitory nature of such beauty makes our hearts weep, even as they rejoice.

When such a sound brings us a hymn written for children, with a text describing the birth of a child, the poignancy grows exponentially. No wonder God, after trying to reach God's people through prophets, priests, and sages, finally broke into human time as an infant. God recognized that the power of childhood to rouse our apathy and pierce our cynicism was a mighty weapon of love.

It still is. We have very different views of childhood from the Victorians, but the fact remains that the soul of the child still sings to us of newness and possibility. Looking into the clear eyes of an infant, or hearing a choirboy (or, now, thankfully, a choirgirl as well) refreshes our souls. There is an "otherness" to such innocence; somehow, they seem to us closer to God than we are. One little girl I taught once told me about something that had happened before she was born by beginning, "When I was still with Jesus," and it sometimes does indeed seem as if children were someplace else before they came into our human families, and, like Jesus, had "come down to earth from heaven." No wonder that our first celebration of Christmas happens promptly at 10:00 A.M. on Christmas Eve!

Hymn 156

Ride on! ride on in majesty!

Henry Hart Milman (1791–1868)

Henry Hart Milman was the son of the physician to George III. He received his education at Eton and at Brasenose College in Oxford, where he was awarded prizes for his poetry, and where Reginald Heber was among his close friends. After ordination, he spent three years as vicar of St. Mary's, Reading, but he left parish ministry when he was appointed professor of poetry at Oxford. He introduced German biblical-critical techniques of historical research in his *History of the Jews*, the "first English book to . . . use the Bible as an historical source-book without denying its special status as revelation."[6] In 1835, he became rector of St. Margaret's, London, and canon of Westminster, and continued there until he was made dean of St. Paul's Cathedral in 1849. He died in London in 1868 and was buried in St. Paul's.

Milman's hymn about Jesus' entry into Jerusalem (Mt.21:1–9; Mk.11:1–10; Lk.19:28–38; Jn:12:12–16) first appeared in his friend Reginald Heber's posthumous *Hymns written and adapted to the Weekly Church Service of the Year.* It is said that when Heber received the manuscript of "Ride on" for the collection in which he was trying to include the work of the best living poets, he exclaimed, "A few more hymns like this, and I need not wait for the help of Scott and Southey!"[7] The text also appeared in Milman's own *Selection of Psalms and Hymns* (1837).

"Ride on! ride on in majesty!" is thought to be one of the finest hymns in the English language. Lionel Adey writes, "Blending lucidity and highly conscious art, [Milman's] 'Ride on, ride on in majesty' yields to no hymn in English in its appeal to the whole range of human intelligence and sensitivity."[8] Hymnologist Carol Doran points out that there are no less than twenty-two exclamation marks in this hymn, conveying "a sense of resolute courage in the face of unavoidable tragedy."[9]

The solemn unison tune in *The Hymnal 1982* was composed in 1939 by the Canadian composer Graham George, who wrote:

> It originated as a result of a choir practice before Palm Sunday . . . during which I had been thinking WINCHESTER NEW is a fine tune, but it has nothing whatever to do with the tragic trumpets, as one might theatrically call them, of Palm Sunday. At breakfast the following morning I was enjoying my toast and

> marmalade when the first two lines of this tune sang themselves unbidden into my mind. This seemed too good to miss, so I went to my study, allowed the half-tune to complete itself—which it did with very little trouble—and there it was.[10]

When I was a teenager, our parish youth group would gather during the week before Palm Sunday for an annual project. We would take some of the long palm fronds ordered from some distant land by the Altar Guild, and fold them in such a way that, by the end of our meeting, there was a basket full of palm crosses ready to be given to the congregation on Palm Sunday. It was a sociable time, full of adolescent chatter. Some of the boys would inevitably duel with one another before folding their palms, while the girls kept at our task, despite the fact that our hands would begin to sting from working with the knife-edged fronds.

During that liturgical era in the church, Palm Sunday was a celebratory day. People who came to church on Christmas and Easter would also come on Palm Sunday to "get their palms," which then would be dutifully tucked behind a picture in their bedrooms. We young people liked it because it was a day for processions with rousing hymns. While the palm crosses we had made during our lively youth group meeting gave a hint of the Passion to come, we didn't think much about that. Nor did we really notice all the words of a hymn like "Ride on! ride on in majesty!" On one level, we knew what was to come: Holy Week, with Good Friday at the end. But we didn't think about it much on Palm Sunday. Palm Sunday was the day for parades.

When Good Friday came, with Holy Saturday and Easter on its heels, there would be much talk about the spiritual passage from death to resurrection, and its connection to the events in our lives. But there was never much talk about the other kind of spiritual passage—the passage which occurred between the Entry into Jerusalem and the Garden of Gethsemane, the passage from triumph into desolation.

One of my teachers once said that there is nothing that happens to us that did not happen to Jesus. We have Jesus' companionship in all our life's events, joyous and desolate.

I think we are fortunate in our Palm Sunday liturgy to be able to practice walking with Jesus along the road into Jerusalem, pursuing his path until it reaches the Garden of Gethsemane and the Hill of Golgotha. When we walk that path with him, we will be able to understand more easily that Jesus walks with us, as we ourselves move through the passages from apparent triumph to apparent failure. For that is an inevitable pattern in life.

Who has not known that plunge? Perhaps we love our job and think we are doing good work, and are told one day that we are no longer needed. Perhaps we have given our hearts in love to someone, and discover that they do not love us any more. Perhaps we have trusted someone, and are betrayed. Perhaps we think we are in the bloom of health, and suddenly get bad news from the doctor.

Jesus chose to walk this difficult path with us. He "emptied himself, taking the form of a servant, being born in the likeness of men. And being found in human form he humbled himself and became obedient unto death, even death on a cross." (Phil.2:7–8)

We do not need to wait until Easter to hear good news. We, who need the companionship of Jesus during our own passages from triumph to desolation, already recognize good news on Palm Sunday!

Hymn 168, 169

O sacred head, sore wounded

Paul Gerhardt (1607–1676); tr. Robert Seymour Bridges (1844–1930) and J. W. Alexander (1804–1859)

The career of the beloved German hymnwriter Paul Gerhardt was delayed by the Thirty Years War and by poverty. Finally, at the age of forty-five, he was offered a parish in a small village, was married to the woman he had long loved, and began to publish the hymns he had for many years been writing. The hymns brought him fame and opportunity. When he was called in 1657 as assistant pastor to the great St. Nikolaikirche in Berlin, he became known as a fine preacher and a man of deep piety and good works. However, in 1666, he resigned this post through unwillingness to assent to an edict of the Elector of Brandenburg which forbade free discussion of the differences between the Lutheran and the Reformed Churches. Two years later, he was appointed as archdeacon at Lubben, where he remained until his death.

Although he was theologically a staunch Lutheran, Gerhardt was influenced by Catholic mysticism, especially that of the school of St.

Bernard of Clairvaux. "O sacred head, sore wounded" is based on a Latin text, traditionally attributed to Bernard, but possibly written by Arnulf of Louvain (1200–1250).

The hymn is a free translation of the final part of a poem of seven parts, to be sung on different days of the week. Captioned a "rhythmical prayer to the various members of Christ's body suffering and hanging on the Cross," the poem addresses in turn Jesus' feet, knees, hands, sides, breast, heart, and head. Whether or not composed by Bernard, the poem reflects the type of religious life he exemplified, combining a mystic faith and an emotional intensity that enabled him to lead kings, emperors, and popes.

Paul Gerhardt's translation of *Salve Caput cruentatum* was in turn paraphrased in English by former British poet laureate Robert Bridges (st.1–3 and 5) and American Presbyterian minister and scholar James Waddell Alexander (st.4). Thus, the hymn is the product of three different centuries, four different countries, and four different religious traditions, probably making it the most ecumenical of all hymns in popular use!

The tune with which the text is indelibly associated, PASSION CHORALE, was originally a German love song, "My Heart is Distracted by a Gentle

Maid," first appearing in a 1601 collection of songs by Hans Leo Hassler. Hassler's tune is harmonized by Johann Sebastian Bach, who must have been especially fond of the Passion Chorale: it appears five times in his "St. Matthew Passion," twice in the "Christmas Oratorio," in five cantatas, and in a chorale prelude for organ. Brahms also used the melody in two chorale preludes for organ.

Think of all the depictions of the crucifixion you have seen throughout your life. Because Jesus' observant Jewish disciples took seriously the second commandment—"Thou shalt not make to thyself any graven image"—we have no drawings of the actual event. Artists across the centuries have had to imagine it. And in painting or sculpting their versions of that scene on Golgotha, they have created a visual theology. These images revealed their beliefs about Jesus' death, and suggested a great deal about their own spiritual needs, as well.

I think of early icons of the crucifixion, in which Jesus is portrayed objectively as a timeless figure, a window through which the viewer can glimpse eternity. I think of the proud images of

"Christus Rex," the King who conquered evil in the great struggle on the cross. I think of other crucifixes: the limp and beautiful body hanging on polished wood over a prie-dieu, or the strong carpenter carved by a contemporary sculptor, looking courageously toward the west end of a convent chapel I know.

But when I sing this hymn, I think of the crucifixion depicted on the Isenheim triptych. Painted by the early sixteenth-century German artist Grünewald for the hospital chapel of St. Anthony's monastery in Isenheim, the centerpiece is the contorted body of the suffering Jesus. The fingers of his nail-pierced hands are splayed like great claws against a dark sky. The neck is absolutely limp, the sacred head, wounded with thorns, hangs heavily on his chest. The flesh is pock-marked, almost rotting.

On one side of the cross, Mary, rigid with horror, is held, fainting, in the arms of the beloved disciple John, and a grieving Magdalene reaches out in prayer. On the other side stands John the Baptist, carrying a prophetic book and gesturing towards his cousin.

There is no beauty in this crucifixion: "so marred was his appearance, beyond human semblance." (Isa.52:14) He has "no form or majesty that we should look at him, nothing in his appearance that we should desire him." (Isa.53:2) This crucifixion is shocking. It is the real human face of suffering and death, neither idealized nor prettified.

I remind myself that this crucifixion was painted for a hospital chapel, where mortally ill people would be seeing it. Here was a lifeless Jesus to whom they could relate, when their own bodies were failing them. Here was a Jesus, who, by not masking the horrors of death, helped to banish its terror for the dying. This was a Jesus whose contorted body mirrored their own agonies of pain. Here was the Jesus they needed, their companion in the dreaded passage at life's end.

We all need to look at this Jesus once in a while, no matter what our preference in crucifixes, because this Jesus is the truth. This is the human Jesus, whose flesh was as mortal as ours. This is the human Jesus, who did not call legions of angels to his rescue, but went through it all, right up to the last death rattle. If we can be with him in this Passiontide hymn, it will be easier to know that he is with us, when our day comes as well.

Hymn 199,200

Come, ye faithful, raise the strain

John of Damascus (8th cent.); tr. John Mason Neale (1818–1866)

John of Damascus is revered as a major theologian of the Eastern church and one of her greatest hymnwriters. John was born into a wealthy family; his father, Mansur, a Christian of Damascus, was chief financial adviser to the Caliph Abd-el-Melik. He and his foster brother Cosmas were educated by a Sicilian monk of great learning who had been captured by pirates in a raid on Italy and brought to the slave market in Damascus. Mansur secured his release and adopted him also as a son.

On the death of his father, John was made chief councillor to the Caliph, but his faith compelled him to abandon his office, to give away all his possessions, and to withdraw with his brother to the great monastery of Sabas, or Mar Saba, carved into the face of a cliff in the desert near Jerusalem, where he became a priest.

John's theological works, especially his classic *Fount of Wisdom*, exercised a considerable influence on later theologians, especially the thirteenth-century Scholastics. He defended the use of icons in the controversy with the Iconoclasts or "image-breakers," writing three discourses on the subject between 726 and 730. He was declared a Doctor of the Church by Pope Leo XIII in 1890.

In hymnology, he was a chief exponent of the new form called the canon, and wrote a number of these for the great festivals of the church. His role in organizing the chants of the liturgy in the Eastern church is often likened to the role of Gregory the Great in organizing the music of the Western church. He is credited with the setting down of the *Ocotechnos*, a book of chants in the eight *echoi* or modes, for the festivals of the liturgical year.

A Greek canon (unlike our present-day use of the word) is a type of poetry which is based generally on a biblical canticle, such as the Song of Moses in Ex. 15:1–18, the Song of Hannah in 1 Sam. 2:1–10, or the *Benedicite* in Dan. 3:27–33. A canon is invariably acrostic in structure, sometimes alphabetical, and sometimes spelling out a verse of poetry, a quotation, or the name of the author.

"Come, ye faithful, raise the strain" is the first ode of the canon for St. Thomas's Sunday (Easter 1). It is based on the "Song of Moses" and vividly compares and relates the deliverance effected by Moses with that effected by Christ.

The translation by John Mason Neale appeared first as an illustration in an article on "Greek Hymnology" in the *Christian Remembrancer* for April 1859, and later appeared in his collection *Hymns of the Eastern Church*, 1862.

Neale was educated at Trinity College, Cambridge, where, despite his Evangelical roots, he became identified with the Oxford Movement and was one of the founders of a local expression of the movement, known as the Cambridge Camden Society. After ordination, he was unable to accept a parish because of ill health, and spent the next three winters in Madeira, India.

From 1846 until his death, he was warden of Sackville College, East Grinstead, an almshouse for indigent elderly men, at a salary of £28 a year. There, he divided his time between his literary and scholarly activities and the Sisterhood of St. Margaret, which he founded in 1855. This community focused on the education of girls and the care of the sick, and though it at first met with violent opposition—even rioting—from Protestant quarters, it developed into one of the leading religious communities in the Anglican Communion.

Neale's liturgical practices led the Bishop of Chichester to prohibit his priestly duties from 1847 to 1863, but that did not deter him from expressing his commitment to the Oxford Movement. The movement's high regard for the spirituality and practice of the early Christian church was expressed in Neale's many translations of ancient Greek and Latin hymns and his paraphrases of Orthodox texts.

In lines penned during Neale's lifetime, one of his contemporaries wrote, "In his hymn-writing Dr. Neale has headed a new movement. He has attracted the Church to her oldest stores of praise as they are treasured in the Greek and Latin tongues."[11] English hymnody would never be the same again.

Two tunes are provided; one by Arthur Seymour Sullivan (who provided music for W. S. Gilbert's operetta librettos) that has been in the hymnal since 1892, and a rhythmic carollike tune from the sixteenth century.

Early this Easter morning, I have gone on a walk in the nearby woods. The liturgy of the Easter Vigil last night is still vividly with me.

The woods are celebrating Easter, as well. 'Tis the spring of nature as well as of souls today. The quiet Sunday morning is alive with birdsong. Buds are swelling on the ash trees and a few green plants are beginning to poke through the leafy carpet of the forest floor. Underfoot, the earth is what the poet e.e. cummings calls "mud-luscious." The frozen landscape through which I cross-country skied only a few weeks ago is coming to life.

There is, for the first time this year, a subtle haze of greenness. I think of the theologian and scientist Teilhard de Chardin, who speaks of the "diaphany" of God: "the great mystery of Christianity is not exactly the appearance, but the transparence, of God in the universe."[12] The resurrected Christ is shining diaphanously throughout this springtime woods.

The mystic Meister Eckhardt wrote, "Every creature is a word of God and is a book about God." When I read the book of God in nature, it teaches me that Easter is a fundamental reality. Death is transformed into life each spring, whether as rich compost fertilizing the forest floor or as an oak bursting into leaf once again. I rejoice in the freedom of the natural world, in which everything from hawk to horse chestnut is simply itself, without the impediments we humans create which keep us from living out our true identity as children of God.

What can I learn from this word of God in the woods on an Easter morning? As a faithful human being on this lovely planet, I can "raise the strain" of gladness to the Creator. I can respect, and also try to emulate, the integrity of the nonhuman creation, deemed "very good" by God. I can try to remember to read this Scripture of the natural world not only on Easter morning, but regularly, walking through it as a pilgrim, in prayer.

I was the solitary walker this morning in the woods at the edge of our town. I was almost at the end of the path when I saw someone. It was a college student, perhaps a member of the cross-country team, wearing shorts and a tee shirt on this spring morning. He, also, became part of my contemplation of God's word in nature. Like the Resurrection appearances of Jesus, this young man in white reminded me that we carry God's life within us, and that it is ever renewed, ever eternal.

Hymn 207

Jesus Christ is risen today

Latin, 14th cent.; tr. Lyra Davidica, 1708; St. 4, Charles Wesley (1707–1788)

"Jesus Christ is risen today" is based on the nine-stanza hymn *Surrexit Christus hodie,* which was found in three fourteenth-century manuscripts from Prague, Engleberg, and Munich.

The Latin hymn is a trope on the *Benedicamus Domino*, which was sung at the end either of the Easter Mass or the Easter offices. "Troping"—making additions to the authorized text and music of the liturgy—was popular during the Middle Ages. The practice expanded to such an extent that the Council of Trent (1545–1563) ultimately abolished all embellishments to the liturgy with the exception of five authorized sequences.

A three-stanza English translation first appeared in *Lyra Davidica, or a Collection of Divine Songs and Hymns, partly New Composed, partly Translated from the High German and Latin Hymns: and set to easy and pleasant tunes, for more General Use*, published in London by a famous music printer, John Walsh, in 1708. The fourth stanza, a doxology written by Charles Wesley, was added in 1862.

The melody for the text made its first appearance in *Lyra Davidica*, where the anonymous author made the comment that the purpose of the tunes in the book was to provide "a little freer air than the grave movement of the Psalm-tunes."[13]

We once lived a few miles from a Russian Orthodox seminary, so that for several years I was able to celebrate Easter twice. The first one was at my suburban parish church at mid-morning on Easter Day. The familiar Easter hymns, the chorales and fanfares by visiting brass players, the special choir anthems, the Easter finery, the familiar faces, and the insistence of the preacher that the congregation shout "The Lord is risen indeed! Alleluia" when he proclaimed "Alleluia. Christ is risen!"—all spelled "Easter the way I have always known it."

My second Easter celebration usually occurred a week later at the Russian Orthodox Seminary, thanks to the discrepancy between the Eastern and Western liturgical calendars. On the Orthodox Easter Even, I stood in the midst of the congregation of St. Vladimir's, holding candles in the icon-lined seminary chapel. I knew very few people in the congregation, most of whom had broad Slavic faces.

The celebration lasted virtually the whole night long, beginning with the Easter offices. Immediately before the reading of the gospel, the chapel emptied, the door was shut, and a candlelit procession wove through the seminary garden. Back at the chapel door, the deacon read the gospel, the crucifer struck the door with his cross, and we gained entry in order to join the foretaste of the celestial banquet, mirrored here on earth so elaborately in this chapel on Easter Even. The general shape of the liturgy matched that in my Episcopal parish church, but the atmosphere had an exoticism and mystery that made these some of the most memorable Easter celebrations of my life. I can still hear the crowded chapel reverberating repeatedly with the Easter proclamation—"The Lord is risen! Indeed he has risen!" in English, Russian, and Greek, and without any prompting from the clergy. Morning was beginning to dawn when I made my way home, weary and exhilarated.

Since those days, I have had a few occasions to celebrate the Easter Vigil at a monastery or convent. After a few hours sleep, we rose while it was still dark, so that the igniting of the new fire was literally the first light. As the lessons were read, the sky began to lighten, until finally, at daybreak, the Eucharist began, and we were fed with the food of the Risen Lord.

These liturgies, it must be admitted, can be exhausting—perhaps, most of all, those at St. Vladimir's, where there were no pews or chairs. But the long nights of prayer and readings prepared us for a daybreak that was more than just the rising of the sun in the East. It was the blindingly joyous light of the rising of the Son.

"Jesus Christ is risen today!" "Alleluia! Christ is risen. The Lord is risen indeed. Alleluia!"

Hymn 225 (Also 175 and 216)

Hail thee, festival day

Venantius Honorius Fortunatus (540?–600?)

Venantius Honorius Fortunatus, born near Treviso in northern Italy, was converted to Christianity at an early age, and educated in rhetoric, grammar and law at Ravenna, then under Byzantine rule. When Fortunatus developed a severe eye disease which threatened blindness, he is said to have recovered his sight after anointing his eyes with oil from a lamp burning before the altar of St. Martin of Tours in Ravenna. In thanksgiving for his recovery, he set out on a pilgrimage to St. Martin's shrine in Tours. He was to spend most of the rest of his adult life in Gaul.

There, he was soon to meet the Frankish Queen Rhadegonda, who had been captured in battle and forced to wed the Frankish King Clotaire I. Eventually separating from her husband, she founded an abbey at Poitiers; an avid collector of relics, she secured from Justin II, the Byzantine emperor, a relic of the True Cross for the abbey. She named her abbey Sainte Croix, in honor of this gift from Constantinople.

She and Fortunatus became friends, and she persuaded him to take holy orders and to enter the abbey. Fortunatus was to became Bishop of Poitiers in 599, not long before his death.

During his lifetime, Fortunatus produced numerous poetic writings, ranging from rhymes thanking his hosts for dinner to some of the finest poetry in Christendom.

Fortunatus wrote his 110-line Latin poem *Tempora florigero rutilant distincta sereno* between the years 567 and 576, in honor of the baptism at an Easter Vigil of the newly converted Saxons by Felix, Bishop of Nantes. The poem had three themes: the celebration of the awakening of nature in spring; the work of salvation, which included a welcome to Easter Day and a prayer to Christ; and concluding tributes and charges to Felix.

The poem quickly became popular and was adapted for singing. Various portions of the poem, each beginning with lines thirty-nine and forty—*Salva festa dies toto venerabilis aevo / Qua Deus infernum vicit et astra tenet*—were produced as processionals for Easter, Ascension, Pentecost, Corpus

Christi, and other festal occasions. Eventually, new hymns, using only the first line of the original, were written. This process of making a new text out of selections from other literary and musical works is called "centonization," so these versions of *Salva festa dies* are called "centos."

The Hymnal 1982 contains three "centos" from Fortunatus's poem: for Easter, Ascension Day, and Pentecost.

According to hymnologist Ruth Ellis Messenger, the first and third stanzas of Hymn 175, the Easter version, may be the earliest instance in which a hymnwriter compares Jesus' Resurrection to the renewal of nature in the spring.[14] Stanzas two and four sketch the story of the Crucifixion and Resurrection; stanzas five, six, and seven are prayers to the Trinity for health, protection, forgiveness, light, life, and peace.

The images are triumphant ones, of Jesus "treading the pathway of death" to bestow life on humanity, of a Creator who rules earth and heavens, and of the Spirit of life and of power. They help us to understand the events of the gospel through the eyes of the renowned Fortunatus, Bishop of Poitiers, who could be said to be the last Roman and first medieval hymnwriter.

Hymn 216, the Ascension version, while omitting the two stanzas concerning the Resurrection, is almost identical to the Easter version. Only the refrain, dating from no later than the twelfth century, is unique to the Ascension version. In both these versions, the translations are a composite from three authors: Maurice Bell, Percy Dearmer, and George Gabriel Scott Gillet, who used versions of Fortunatus's hymn found in early processionals from Sarum and York.

Hymn 225, the Pentecost version, uses the first line of Fortunatus's poem. The fourth stanza echos the prayers to the Spirit in the other versions. The remainder of the text, found in the York Processional, is by an unknown author who lived no later than the fourteenth century. The translator is George Gabriel Gillet. The poem describes the events of Pentecost as found in Acts 2:1–11, with an allusion to Paul's list of the sevenfold gifts of the Spirit in 1 Cor.12:7–11.

The tune for *Salva festa dies* was composed by Ralph Vaughan Williams for the *English Hymnal* (1906). It originally appeared anonymously, but was finally credited to the composer in *Songs of Praise* (1931).

When our children were small, in the quiet time of conversation at bedtime, we began to develop a small liturgy. It went like this:

> Question: "What shall we talk about?"
> Answer: "Let's talk about birthdays."

In the spectrum of exciting topics at bedtime, birthdays were always a winner. We discussed the details long in advance, from the requirement for orange frosting on the cake when one of our sons was going through his orange-is-my-favorite-color stage, to the traditional peanut hunt and game of musical chairs and the hoped-for presents.

It is not only children who like to talk about birthdays. Adult members of our families also mark the passage of the years with special celebrations—of graduations, marriages, and wedding anniversaries.

I rejoice that we like to "talk about birthdays" in church, too. The church's feast days remind us that God enters history. When we celebrate a baby's birth in the dark days of December, we remind ourselves that the Incarnation is not merely an abstract concept, but a historic event. When we deck our altars with Easter lilies on a springtime Sunday and shout out "Alleluia," we are celebrating not just the concept of Resurrection but the "day whereon Christ arose, breaking the kingdom of death." When we extinguish the Paschal Candle on Ascension Day, we remind ourselves that Jesus was standing with his disciples on a particular hilltop in Bethany, as his physical presence on earth ended and his eternal reign in heaven began.

When we wear red on Pentecost, the "birthday of the Church," we are remembering an actual gathering in a room suddenly filled with the rush of a mighty wind and tongues of fire.

The liturgical cycle of the church year reminds us not only that Jesus' life was sacred history, but that our lives are sacred history as well. God works through our stories. God is the creator of the recurrent cycles of the earth, but God is also the inventor of linear time—from birth to death, from Christmas to Pentecost. Our celebrations are reminders of that fact. Let's talk about birthdays.

Hymn 287

For all the saints, who from their labors rest

William Walsham How (1823–1897)

William Walsham How wrote the text of "For all the saints" in 1864, for use on All Saints Day. It was originally entitled "Saints Day Hymn—Cloud of Witnesses—Heb. 12:1" and intended as a commentary on "I believe in the communion of saints."

William How was an Anglican clergyman who ministered in several cures in rural England, became chaplain of the English Church in Rome, Suffragan Bishop of East London, and the first Bishop of Wakefield, and was particularly known for his work on behalf of the poor in the east end of London. Affectionately known as "the poor man's bishop," he is reported to have declined the bishopric of Manchester without even bothering to tell his family, and later refused the same post at Durham, a position that would have doubled his salary.

He once wrote a description of the ideal minister of the Gospel: "Such a minister should be a man pure, holy, and spotless in his life; a man of much prayer; in character meek, lowly, and infinitely compassionate; of tenderest love to all; full of sympathy for every pain and sorrow, and devoting his days and nights to lightening the burdens of humanity."[15] People who knew him said it was almost a perfect description of How himself, who had engraved on his pastoral staff the saying of St. Bernard: *Pasce verbo, pasce vita* ("Feed with the Word; feed with the life.")

He was also a champion of ecumenism and of liberal theology within the Anglican Church. Attempting to reconcile science and the Bible, he wrote, "Evolution is the wonderful way in which the Lord formed man out of the dust of the ground."

How received honorary doctorates from the Archbishop of Canterbury in 1879 and from Oxford in 1886. He died while vacationing in Ireland, and was greatly mourned by those he directly served, as well as by the Christian church at large, for he had become known for his writings, which included about fifty-four hymns. His hymns embody an ideal he once expressed: "A good hymn should be like a good prayer—simple, real, earnest, and reverent."[16]

Ralph Vaughn Williams wrote the tune expressly for How's text in 1906. At first it was criticized by some as being "jazz music"; now it is considered to be one of the finest hymn-tunes written during the twentieth century.

I have sung this hymn every All Saints' Day, remembering the great saints of the church who are part of the "great company of heaven." Just as I remember my friends, family, and mentors with gratitude and affection on their birthdays, so on this day I think of my favorite saints. We all probably have our favorites—saints who have stepped off their pedestals or out of their stained glass windows—and come to life for us.

On All Saints' Day, I celebrate some of these companions who have guided me over the years with their insights. The saints of the early church have left their legacy in the Gospels, the Epistles, and the stories of the martyrs. But I also think of some soul-sisters who lived after Biblical times: the visionary Hildegard of Bingen, a renaissance woman long before the Renaissance; Julian of Norwich, who saw a loving God in all that exists; the irrepressible Teresa of Avila, reformer and mystic. I think of my brothers in Christ: Francis of

Assisi, who sang a canticle of Creation both with his poem and with his life; and John of the Cross, who sought Love in the soul's dark night.

I think of those who have not been awarded official sainthood, but are also God's blessed ones. I think of George Herbert in the seventeenth century, the faithful pastor and poet. I remember Evelyn Underhill, the scholarly and quiet teacher of prayer.

I think also of Desmond Tutu, whom I met when he visited Trinity Church, Wall Street. A small man, he became ten feet tall when he preached. Although I knew he was a man of courage and often risked his physical safety for the cause of justice, the most remarkable thing about him was his ebullience, and a smile that lit up the world around him. Desmond Tutu was totally there. Once, when I asked him to sign one of his books for me before a service, he wrote with such attention to what he was doing that he didn't notice that the entire procession was waiting for him to finish.

Elaine Ramshaw writes:

> One of the tasks of the church, in its liturgical life as well as in its formal education, is to recall the history of humanity in a different

> way than is usual in secular society. The church . . . remembers a different sort of hero.
>
> . . . Rather than see such people as human-interest sidebar stories in a history focused on the wielders of power, the liturgical calendar puts them in center stage of the history that matters.[17]

I am glad that we recognize that the saints—both the Saints we honor in our Church Year and the saints who cross our paths—should be in center stage. Perhaps that is the reason this hymn is frequently used at funerals. Its images of endurance and victory seem especially appropriate for those faithful Christians whose final years have, because of illness or extreme old age, been a struggle. They, also, deserve a song of praise, and a final "Alleluia!"

Hymn 290

Come, ye thankful people, come
Henry Alford (1810–1871)

Henry Alford was born in London, the son of the rector of Aston Sandford, Buckinghamshire. At the age of six he wrote a life of Paul, and at ten a pamphlet *Looking Unto Jesus the Believers' Support Under Trials and Afflictions*. He compiled his first hymnbook at eleven and openly dedicated his life to God on the flyleaf of his Bible at sixteen: "I do this day, in the presence of God and my own soul, renew my covenant with God, and solemnly determine henceforth to become his, and to do his work as far as in me lies."[18]

Alford graduated with honors from Trinity College, Cambridge, and was ordained the following year to the curacy of Ampton, Alford, where he assisted his father and began boarding and tutoring private pupils. He served as vicar of Wymeswold (1835–1853) and incumbent at Quebec Chapel in London (1853–1857) and finally, in 1857, was appointed dean of Canterbury Cathedral, where he served until his death.

Meanwhile, he published forty-eight books, the most notable being a four-volume commentary on the Greek New Testament, which required some twenty years of preparation and which served as a standard critical commentary during the last half of the nineteenth century. He also composed keyboard and vocal music and founded a choral society for the presentation of oratorios in Canterbury Cathedral.

"Come, ye thankful people, come" is considered one of finest harvest hymns in all hymnody. It first appeared in *Psalms and Hymns, adapted for the Sundays and Holidays throughout the year* (1844), while Alford was in charge of a rural parish where the autumn Harvest Home festival was a major event. At that time overland transport was so poor that a local crop failure presaged a winter of misery. Richard Blackmore's classic *Lorna Doone* describes in Chapter Twenty-nine the kind of community celebration that would involve this kind of hymn; in some places, each family contributed one sheaf of grain towards making bread for the ensuing year's communion services.

The hymn has been a great favorite at harvest festivals in England and for Thanksgiving services in the United States. The harvest to which Alford alludes in the last three stanzas is the consummation of history as depicted in Jesus' explanation of his parable of the weeds in the wheat in

Mt.13:36–43. The fourth stanza begins with an echo of Rev. 22:20: "The one who testifies to these things says, 'Surely I am coming soon.' Amen. Come, Lord Jesus!"

The text and tune for this hymn have been matched in hymnals since 1871.

Autumn is a beautiful season in northern Ohio. The farmland which surrounds our small town is no longer green with growth; the fields, framed by trees afire with yellow and red, glow with gold and brown under the autumn sun. Some trees have already shed their leaves and reveal the fractal geometry of their branches. The texture of the landscape has come into high relief.

The labor of the summer is a thing of the past. The land is at rest. The harvest is over, and families gather to celebrate nature's abundance, around tables groaning under platters turkey, squash, mashed potatoes, cranberry sauce, and pies of every description. There is a feeling of closure and comfort, a pause in the turning of the year.

I am not a farmer, but we do tend a plot of vegetables at the back of our garden. We have given part of the space to raspberries and strawberries, and eagerly await the first juicy specimens each year. A year ago, I planted an asparagus bed, and, because we have been warned that allowing the plants to mature for the first couple of years increases their vigor, we have to content ourselves with watching the delectable spears become feathery fronds. By now, the last tomatoes have been eaten or frozen, and from our basil I have made a dozen batches of pesto to remind us of summer in the midst of the months ahead.

The cycle in our garden takes my breath away. The first shoots of the asparagus in the springtime, the strawberries and raspberries coming to life again, the basil seeds I have planted poking up their first tender leaves, all fill me with wonder. The ripening fruits of late summer overwhelm me with the lushness of nature. Then the poignancy of autumn arrives, and nature begins to shed everything but the essentials.

My garden teaches me about life and helps me raise the song of my own harvest-home: the wonder of life's beginnings; the slow growth toward maturity; the abundant middle years; the ripening of the final third of life; and the final shedding of all that is not essential. The garden teaches me that death is not an end, but a harvest: the goal of all our seasons. Whether we sing of the end of the gardening season, the end of our individual lives, or the end of time, the process is in the hands of God.

> Even so, Lord, quickly come
> to thy final harvest-home;
> gather thou thy people in,
> free from sorrow, free from sin;
> there, for ever purified,
> in thy presence to abide;
> come, with all thine angels come,
> raise the glorious harvest-home.

Hymn 324

Let all mortal flesh keep silence

Liturgy of St. James; para. Gerard Moultrie (1829–1885)

The Liturgy of St. James is an ancient liturgy, existing in both a Greek and Syrian form. It is traditionally ascribed to James, the brother of Jesus and the first Bishop of Jerusalem. The liturgy became traditional in the Syriac-, Armenian-, and

Georgian-speaking part of the church. In certain Orthodox churches, it is still used on October 23, the day the Eastern church commemorates St. James's death, as well as on the Sunday after Christmas.

In the fifth-century form of the Liturgy of St. James, this "Cherubic Hymn" was used at the presentation of the sacred elements at the time of the offertory. It was later adopted for inclusion in the Liturgy of St. Basil, the standard liturgy of Greek Orthodoxy, for use on Easter Eve.

The metrical translation was composed by Gerard Moultrie for the second edition of *Lyra Eucharistica*. Born in Rugby, England, the son of the rector of Rugby parish, Moultrie was educated at Rugby School and at Exeter College, Oxford. He held various chaplaincies and spent most of his life as vicar of Southleigh and warden of St. James' College, Southleigh. He wrote much religious verse and many hymns, both original compositions and translations from Greek, Latin, and German.

The text was matched with a seventeenth-century French carol arranged by Ralph Vaughan Williams, one of the editors of the *English Hymnal*.

I will never forget my first silent retreat. In my final year before college, I went to visit a convent in Catonsville, Maryland, where a high school friend of mine had been raised by the sisters in the adjoining children's home which they tended.

Entering the convent grounds was like stepping into a great ocean of peace. The sisters habitually went about their work quietly, and the "Great Silence" spanned the night from after Compline, the final evening office, to after breakfast.

During the day or so I was on retreat, I did not speak at all. I felt myself relaxing into the silence like a swimmer floating in salt water. It was as if the silence supported and surrounded me as I plunged into the ocean that was God.

Silence is still necessary for my journey. Our home is a quiet one, although it was not always so when our children were young. Since my husband and I both take a while to become alert in the morning, we do not talk much over the breakfast table. At some time during the day, I need time alone in my study, to pray, to reflect, and to write, and the day does not go well if I have missed this time.

I do not think that I am unique in needing times when my "mortal flesh keeps silence." Certainly, the great masters of prayer have taught the necessity for silence. This, of course, is the essence of contemplative prayer: to be still in the presence of God.

While some people are more adept at praying with words, even in verbal prayer there is the need to stop every once in a while to listen, as well. Even in the prayer in which we ponder a passage of Scripture, there are times when we need to pause and sit quietly, so that the words and images can reverberate within us and God can speak to us through them.

Outward silence is merely a sign of the silence that we can carry within us. The movement of "Hesychasm" in the Eastern Orthodox church, the origins of which extend back to the fourth and fifth centuries, teaches that silence and peace can be our constant companions, no matter how busy our lives.

We discover this silence when we discover that the Source of our being can be found within us. Hesychasm teaches its disciples to find it through the continual reciting of a prayer to Jesus. But there are many other ways to "Be still and know that I am God." (Ps. 46:11) We can be attentive to our breathing, both when we are at prayer and when we go about our lives, remembering that God is the source of our life. We can take time for a quiet walk in the woods or the park. We can, paradoxically, listen to music, not as background but as a focus of our attention.

Silence not only gives our souls an opportunity to expand and breathe. It also is our best—and sometimes only—response to the mystery of God.

This is true both in our personal prayer and in our worship, when observing periods of silence helps us join the ranks of the host of heaven in praising the God for whom we will never have adequate words.

Hymn 339

Deck thyself, my soul, with gladness

Johann Franck (1618–1677); tr. Catherine Winkworth (1827–1878)

Johann Franck was born in Guben, Germany, the son of a lawyer. His father died when he was only two, and Franck's uncle, the town judge, adopted him and provided him with an excellent education. His uncle eventually sent him to study law at the University of Königsberg, the only German university left undisturbed by the Thirty Years War. Student life there was apparently extremely lively, but it did not distract the young Franck: "his religious spirit, his love of nature, and his friendship with such men as Simon Dach and Heinrich Held [also a hymnwriter], preserved him from sharing in the excesses of his fellow-students."[19]

He returned home two years later at the urgent request of his mother, who, fearful because of the presence in Guben of both Swedish and Saxon troops, wished to have him nearby. Soon he began practice as a lawyer; he became burgess and councillor, then burgomaster. Eventually he was appointed deputy to the Landtag (Diet) of Lower Lusatia.

Despite his successful career, however, Franck's fame today rests on his gifts as a poet rather than on his abilities as a lawyer. In 1877, to mark the bicentenary of his death, a monumental plaque honoring his memory was placed on the outer wall of Guben's Stadtkirche.

During his lifetime, one hundred of Franck's hymns were published. They reflect a transition in German hymnody: from the objective church song of earlier Reformation hymnody to hymns of a more subjective nature.

This classic German Lutheran eucharistic text by Johann Franck first appeared in the author's *Hundert-Thönigue Vater-Unsers-Harffe,* published in Wittenberg in 1646, where the first line, *Schmücke dich, O liebe Seele* was cited. Three years later, a single stanza appeared in print, along with Johann Crüger's magnificent melody. Eight more stanzas were added in the fifth edition of Crüger's *Praxis Pietatis Melica,* published in Berlin in 1653. Later, in his 1674 volume *Geistliches Sion,* Franck gave it the title "Preparation for Holy Communion."

The text is typical of the devotional poetry emphasizing the relationship between the individual and Jesus so characteristic of the period during and after the devastation of the Thirty Years War (1618–1648). It has been suggested that Franck's poem was influenced by Thomas Aquinas's eucharistic hymn, *Lauda Sion Salvatorum,* which also consists of lines of eight syllables.

The text in *The Hymnal 1982* is a modification of the translation by Catherine Winkworth that first appeared in *The Chorale Book for England* (1863). Winkworth could be considered the English language's foremost translator of German hymnody. Born in London, she spent much of her life in Manchester and Bristol, where she promoted women's higher education through the Clifton Association and helped found Clifton College. Her scholarship took the form not only of hymn translations but of research: her book *Christian Singers of Germany* traces the history of the German Chorale. She died suddenly of heart disease in France.

Bishop Percival, headmaster of Clifton College, said of her,

> She was a person of remarkable intellectual and social gifts and very unusual attainments but what specially distinguished her was her combination of rare ability and great knowledge with a certain tender and sympathetic refinement which constitutes the special charm of the womanly character.[20]

A tablet on the wall of Bristol Cathedral honors her, stating that Winkworth "opened a new source of light, consolation, and strength in many thousand homes."[21]

One of the church's most beloved eucharistic hymns, "Deck thyself, my soul, with gladness" was included in *The Hymnal 1940*, reflecting the historical bond between Lutherans and the Church of England and responding to the growing ecumenical movement.

The poem is matched with Crüger's beautiful chorale setting written especially for Franck's text.

In Jesus' parable of the marriage feast in Matthew's gospel, there is a "coda" about the arrival of a "man who had no wedding garment." (Matthew 22:11) I'd always wondered what that wedding garment might be like, until I began to ponder the text of Johann Franck's beautiful eucharistic hymn. The poet gives me the answer: the "wedding garment" we are to wear at the wedding banquet in eternity, as well as in the celestial banquet on earth that is the Eucharist, is the garment of gladness.

I think that most of us have had the experience of arriving at an event and realizing we were dressed inappropriately. I went to college during the late 1950s in a small Midwestern town; when we were invited to a dance, we wore strapless tulle gowns reaching almost to the floor, often with a wisp of additional tulle over our shoulders; on the dance floor, we all looked like members of a corps de ballet. Soon after I graduated and returned to my home town in the New York suburbs, I was invited to a party for recent college graduates at the local Woman's Club. Happily decked in my finery, I arrived at the party site only to find that eastern fashions had changed in my absence, and that the other women were wearing sophisticated cocktail dresses. Dancing in my full gown, which had previously made me feel like a princess, now made me feel like Mrs. Rip Van Winkle, uneasy in this room full of contemporaries who were, unlike me, up to date.

I see examples of this kind of thing occasionally in the concerts we attend here in our musical college town. Once in a while, someone does not get the message. Everyone in the chorus wears black, with the exception of the alto who forgot, and stands radiant in a white blouse and dark skirt. Or every orchestral player has agreed to wear informal concert clothes, except for the oboist who did not pay attention and arrives in a tuxedo.

Wearing the wrong clothing creates some momentary embarrassment. But how about our souls? In the coda to Jesus' parable about the wedding feast, the consequences are more dire: not temporary humiliation but eternal exile!

What is the soul's clothing code in the Eucharist, that meal which is a foretaste of the celestial wedding banquet? And what kind of clothing is inappropriate, or makes us feel as if we do not fit in?

If I had had access to a video link with the Woman's Club on that day so many years ago, I would have been able to observe the other women there and to realize that my dress would not have fit in. If the alto and the oboist had similar technology, they would not have been the unintentional, though brief, focus of the audience's amused attention.

But we can "see" the other guests at God's banquet before we get there. We gather there, at the altar, in the company of the communion of saints, those blessed ones who know that the kingdom of God belongs to the poor, and that at God's table the hungry are satisfied and the sorrowful are able to laugh. Those blessed ones know that even being excluded from human society can never dilute their joy, and that no one is ever turned away from this gathering of God's guests because of what they are wearing.

The only ones who are uncomfortable there are the ones whose souls are decked with attire—like hatred, greed, and violence—that became out-of-date the instant the Good News was proclaimed. The only way to fit in to this party is to leave those old styles behind and to choose a new wardrobe: the gladness of the daylight's splendor, wondrous joy, and gratitude overflowing like a fountain because we are God's beloved guests.

Hymn 362

Holy, holy, holy!
Reginald Heber (1783–1826)

Reginald Heber was a child of good fortune and intellect, born into a home of wealth and culture. At Oxford, he won two prizes for poetry; he was ordained after graduation and became rector in the little village of Hodnet in Shropshire, set in an idyllic pastoral landscape which is reflected in his poetry. One of his aims was to improve the singing in his church; he wrote to a friend "My Psalm-singing continues bad. Can you tell me where I can purchase Cowper's *Olney Hymns* to put in the seats? Some of them I admire much, and any novelty is likely to become a favorite and draw more people to join in the singing."[22] Since he did not find the hymns he wanted anywhere, he finally resolved to create a hymnal of his own, intended to be "appropriate to the Sundays and principal Holydays of the year; connected in some degree with their particular Collects and Gospels, and designed to be sung between the Nicene Creed and the Sermon."[23]

Heber spent his last three years as Bishop of Calcutta, where he died suddenly in a small pool in which he had sought refreshment after preaching a sermon about the evils of the caste system. The collection on which Heber had been working, entitled *Hymns, written and adapted to the Weekly Church Service of the Year*, was published by his widow shortly after his death. It included nine of his own hymns and many contributions by others, among them Milman, Charles Wesley, Arnold, Cowper, Dryden, Addison, Ken and Watts.

"Holy, holy, holy!", the best known of Reginald Heber's hymns, was first published in his *A Selection of Psalms and Hymns for the Parish Church of Banbury*, in the year of his death. A year later, it appeared posthumously in his *Hymns written and adapted to the Weekly Church Service of the Year*.

The hymnologist Percy Dearmer writes that Heber's unusual 11 12.12 10 metre perhaps inaugurated the increasing width of metrical range in later hymnody. He adds:

> It was the more valuable because in the Victorian books there were so few hymns about God; and this, free from all subjectivity, filled a large gap, expressing the pure spirit of worship in stately language. . . .[24]

The hymn's imagery is based on the fourth chapter of the Book of Revelation, in which John describes his vision of the Lamb of God upon a throne before which is "something like a sea of glass, like crystal." (Rev.4:6) In front stand four living creatures, who sing without ceasing, "Holy, holy, holy, the Lord God the Almighty, who was and is and is to come." (Rev.4:8) As the creatures sing, twenty-four elders "worship the one who lives forever and ever; they cast their crowns before the throne." (Rev.4:10)

"Holy, holy, holy" is also the song of the seraphim in Isaiah's vision in Isaiah 6:2–3: "Holy, holy, holy is the Lord of hosts; the whole earth is full of his glory." It is also, of course, the origin of the "Sanctus" in the Eucharist.

Heber's "Holy, holy, holy" was the poet Tennyson's favorite hymn: "Of hymns I like Heber's 'Holy, holy, holy' better than most; and it is in a fine metre too."[25] It was sung at Tennyson's funeral in Westminster Abbey in April 1892.

The music, universally accepted as *the* tune for this text, was written especially for Heber's poem, and is often regarded as the "archetypal Victorian hymn tune."[26]

Erik Routley writes of this hymn:

> In that word "Holy" is epitomized the most august of Old Testament lines of thought and experience. For men of that day, the "holy" was primarily the untouchable. . . . A holy thing was a thing you might not touch; a holy mountain was a mountain you might not climb; a holy place was a place you might not enter . . . [I]n that delicate reticence and courtesy which is part of the texture of the religious life at its most mature, you keep away from something because you love it and feel unworthy to come too near it.[27]

When I was growing up, the only people allowed in the sanctuary of our parish church were the priests, the acolytes, and the members of the altar guild—the only females privileged to go beyond the altar rail, provided they wore blue veils on their heads. This was a place that was so sacred that even kneeling to receive communion sent chills down the spine. When, in my early forties, I became a lay reader and chalice bearer and went beyond the altar rail, it felt at first like breaking a taboo. And yet how I loved doing it!

When I went to seminary, I understood a bit more about what I had experienced, when a professor, in speaking about God, used the phrase, *Mysterium Tremendum et Fascinans,* which is translated, "Mystery both terrifying and fascinating." I, of course, was far from the first to experience both the fear and the attraction of holiness. Even in the Hebrew Scriptures, the holiness of God was a paradox. God was experienced as both awesome and mighty and also as familiar and near. God was too transcendent to be represented in drawing or sculpture, but was personal enough to be represented through stories and word-pictures.

The paradox of God's holiness was made more complex by Jesus, born of a human mother in Bethlehem, and by the event of Pentecost, when it became clear that God was working in the world. In an attempt to describe their experience to the world in a way that others could understand intellectually, the early church struggled with these expressions of the divine holiness and forged the doctrine of the Trinity.

And yet this doctrine remains a challenge. It makes us stretch our intellects to the utmost limit, and conclude that we can never understand the doctrine with our finite minds.

That is why "Holy, holy, holy," does us such a service. As Routley says, it lays ". . . all the emphasis on the wonder and majesty of [the Trinity] and none whatever on the intellectual athleticism of it. . . . The very shakiness and disjointedness in the hymn are a kind of humility." The text, "so magnificently incoherent, so ejaculatory in its diction . . ." clothed in the "mysterious shot-silk colours of the book of Revelation,"[28] accentuates our awe at the holy. We do not need to figure out the doctrine of the Trinity; we need only to sing.

Hymn 370

I bind unto myself today

Att. Patrick (372–466); tr. Cecil Frances Alexander (1818–1895)

Of great antiquity, "I bind unto myself today" has been attributed to St. Patrick since at least the year 690.

St. Patrick was born in Britain to a noble family who had been Christians for at least three generations. When he was sixteen, he was captured by raiders from Ireland, who carried him away to be sold as a slave. He spent the following six years feeding livestock. Patrick eventually escaped, and probably went to study at Lérins, an abbey on a Mediterranean island off the coast of Cannes, between 412–415, at the end of which time he was ordained. In 431, he returned to Ireland as a missionary, and was consecrated Bishop of Ireland the following year. Patrick spent the rest of his life in converting the Irish people to Christianity, which involved not only organizing churches but also contending with the leaders of the native Druidic cult.

"I bind unto myself today" is an example of a Lorica, or "breastplate prayer," to be chanted while dressing oneself or arming for battle.

In the eleventh century manuscripts, the hymn is prefaced by the following story of its origin:

> Patrick made this hymn; in the time of Loegaire mac Neill [the Druidic chief] it was made, and the cause of its composition was for the protection of himself and his monks against the deadly enemies that lay in ambush for the clerics. And it is a lorica of faith for the protection of body and soul against demons and men and vices: when any person shall recite it daily with pious meditation on God, demons shall not dare to face

> him, it shall be a protection to him against all poison and envy, it shall be a guard to him against sudden death, it shall be a lorica for his soul after his decease.
>
> Patrick sang it when the ambuscades were laid for him by Loegaire, in order that he should not go to Tara to sow the Faith, so that on that occasion they were seen before those who were lying in ambush as if they were wild deer having behind them a fawn . . . and "Deer's Cry" is its name.[29]

The Scriptural references include Eph.6:13–14 ("Therefore take up the whole armor of God, so that you may be able to withstand on that evil day, and having done everything, to stand firm. Stand therefore, and fasten the belt of truth around your waist, and put on the breastplate of righteousness.") and 1 Thess.5:8 ("But since we belong to the day, let us be sober, and put on the breastplate of faith and love, and for a helmet the hope of salvation.")

Cecil Frances Alexander wrote the metrical version of Patrick's hymn for the 1891 revision of the *Irish Church Hymnal*. It is paired with two Irish melodies, the stirring ST. PATRICK'S BREASTPLATE and the contrasting DIERDRE.

There are two kinds of protective armor. One kind is represented by the Great Wall of China, built to protect China from her enemies, or the shining armor worn by medieval knights in battles or tournaments. The contemporary versions of that kind of armor are the bombs, guns, and all the pernicious paraphernalia of destruction stockpiled by the nations of the world, and even by some individuals. This kind of armor is meant to protect our bodies from destruction, or at least discourage those who would hurt us.

But does such armor protect the soul?

I know it doesn't work for me. Even when our outward physical safety is assured, most of us sometimes feel vulnerable and afraid. We may feel overwhelmed by the barrage of violent and fearful images we see on the evening news or read in the newspaper. We may feel paralyzed by tragedies in our neighborhood or bad news in our family. It is as if an "enemy" has breached our inner defenses, and we become captive to helplessness.

That is when we realize we need the other kind of armor: the power of the "Lorica": we can bind unto ourselves the strong Name of the Trinity.

There is great power in the images we allow to occupy our minds. When I was a child, I was taken to see the movie *Mrs. Miniver*, and I was terrified by a scene in which a wounded German airman enters Mrs. Miniver's home and holds her at gunpoint. That scene was so memorable that, when I recently saw the movie again, I was in my imagination the frightened little girl who was so sure that the faraway war my parents talked about in hushed voices would one day bring similar soldiers into our kitchen. And then I remembered, equally vividly, a dream I had shortly after seeing the movie over fifty years ago: that the Germans had invaded, and that I had started to say the Lord's Prayer and felt safe and protected.

That is the point of the Lorica. It is not only a prayer for God's protection: it also armors us spiritually with the images of God. The little girl who prayed the "Our Father" in her dream—perhaps drawing on an instinct bequeathed by her Celtic forebears—was able to defend her psyche against fear, even while she slept.

St. Patrick's Lorica of the Holy Trinity teaches us some of the ways to invite God's power to defend our souls: through meditation on the Gospel story, through the companionship of our ancestors in the faith, through our connection with creation, and through dependence on God's fidelity.

But I like to think of a Lorica as any way that helps us weave our awareness of God's presence around our lives "like the Celtic patterns on stones and in the illuminated Gospels."[30] Whether we defend ourselves with St. Patrick's hymn—or the Lord's prayer, a beloved Psalm, a session of Christian yoga or tai chi, a reassuring mantra, or silent contemplation—we have chosen the only armor adequate for the soul's protection. When our souls are afraid, earthly armor will not do; it is prayer alone that can clothe us with the eternal power of the Trinity.

Hymn 401

The God of Abraham praise

Thomas Olivers (1725–1799)

Many individuals have had a share in the history of this hymn, known as the *Yigdal*. The first was Moses Maimonides, the great Hebrew scholar born in Cordoba, Spain, in 1135. In 1148, he fled from Cordoba with his family to escape persecution by the Muslims; the family finally settled in Morocco around 1160. There, Maimonides studied medicine and wrote treatises on the Jewish calendar and on logic.

The family next lived for a while in Alexandria and in Cairo, during which time Maimonides' brother David, a dealer in precious stones, drowned in the Indian Ocean while on a business trip. Maimonides, whose life of study and writing had been supported by his brother, became a physician to support himself, and eventually was appointed physician to the ruler of Egypt.

He soon became famous; according to legend, Richard the Lionhearted once sought his services. Maimonides' two major works are the *Mishnah Torah*, compiled in 1180, and the *Guide*, written in 1190. The *Yigdal* is his summary, in thirteen articles of faith, of the essential articles of Judaism.

A metrical version of this creed has been attributed to Daniel ben Judah, a liturgical poet who lived in Rome in the middle of the fourteenth century. It has been ascribed also to Immanuel ben Solomon, known in Italian as Manoello Guideo, an early fourteenth-century scholar and poet. This version has long been printed in Hebrew prayer books, and it usually is sung antiphonally in synagogues by the cantor and the congregation at the conclusion of the service on the eve of Sabbath and at festivals.

Finally, a Wesleyan preacher from Wales, Thomas Olivers, heard the *Yigdal* sung by Meyer Lyon, otherwise known as *Leoni*, at the Great

Synagogue, Duke's Place, London, and was inspired to write an English version. Olivers is reported to have said, "Look at this; I have rendered it from the Hebrew, giving it, as far as I could, a Christian character, and I have called on Leoni, the Jew, who has given me a synagogue melody to suit it; here is the tune, and it is to be called *Leoni*."[31]

Published in 1772, the hymn was headed "A Hymn to the God of Abraham: in Three Parts: adapted to a celebrated Air, sung by the Priest, Signior Leoni, &c., at the Jews' Synagogue, in London." It became so popular that, by 1799, it had appeared in thirty editions.

The tune is an adaptation of the melody to which the *Yigdal* was sung when Olivers heard it in London.

Thomas Cahill's book *The Gifts of the Jews* is subtitled *How a Tribe of Desert Nomads Changed the Way Everyone Thinks and Feels*.[32] The story of Abraham, he suggests, marked the turning point between two world views.

In the ancient Sumerian civilization, life was understood as cyclical. The wheel of life turned like the high vault of heaven; the gods were as remote as the moon and the stars.

It was in such a setting that, a century or so after the beginning of the second millennium B.C.E., Avram, son of Terrah, heard a voice: "Go from your country and your kindred and your father's house to the land that I will show you. I will make of you a great nation, and I will bless you, and make your name great, so that you will be a blessing." (Gen.12:1–2)

So, *wayyelekh Avram* ("Avram went"). Cahill states that these are

> . . . two of the boldest words in all literature. They signal a complete departure from every thing that has gone before in the long evolution of culture and sensibility. Out of Sumer, civilized repository of the predictable, comes a man who does not know where he is going but goes forth into the unknown wilderness under the prompting of his god.[33]

Eventually, this Avram will be called Abraham, signifying his new status. His name will now mean "the ancestor is exalted," and God will enter into the covenant which is the sign of a new relationship between Abraham's people and their deity.

Avram went. Religion would be no longer what it had been for the Sumerians and other ancient cultures: "impersonal manipulation by means of ritual prescriptions."[34] Instead, in the land of Canaan, a new theology was born. It grew out of a peoples' face-to-face relationship with an inscrutable wilderness God, upon whom they learned they could depend. Human consciousness had been altered, as, for the first time, human beings grasped the fact that they lived in linear history.

It is this God that is praised by three major religions: Judaism, Islam, and Christianity. This is a God who is vast as the terrain through which Abraham and his convoy made their way. This is the great "I AM" who speaks to the humblest soul as well as the greatest Semitic chieftain, the God upon whose oath of covenant love we can depend.

Abraham's God is not one we can tame or manipulate. Praying to this desert deity does not always make us feel comfortable. This God may ask us "to go"—to go beyond our self-interest, our convenience, our fears, our preconceptions about life. Abraham's God helps us walk forward into history—our history. "Enthroned above," this God also walks beside us, through the vast and unknown spaces of the years ahead of each of us.

Hymn 410

Praise, my soul, the King of heaven
Henry Francis Lyte (1793–1847)

Henry Francis Lyte was born in Scotland and received a Bachelor of Arts Degree from Trinity College, Dublin, where he received three poetry prizes. At first, he considered entering the medical profession, but he took holy orders in 1815. After being "jostled from one curacy to another," he became perpetual curate in 1823 of Lower Brixham, Devon, a fishing village, where he was to remain the rest of his life. He was never of robust health, and suffered from asthma and tuberculosis in his late years. Finding the labors of his parish to be undermining his strength, he went to the Continent to regain his health, but died in Nice at the age of fifty-four.

Three volumes of Lyte's poetry were published during his lifetime. "Praise, my soul, the King of heaven," a free paraphrase of Psalm 103, is taken from his collection, *The Spirit of the Psalms* (1834). The volume contained over two hundred eighty paraphrases, written for his congregation in Devon.

In explaining why he wrote his hymns and poems, Lyte expressed himself in these words:

Might verse of mine inspire
One virtuous aim, one high resolve impart—
Light in one drooping soul a hallowed fire,
Or bind one broken heart,

Death would be sweeter then,
More calm my slumber 'neath the silent sod,
Might I thus live to bless my fellowmen,
Or glorify my God.[36]

The tune, composed especially for Lyte's text, is immensely popular and frequently sung at weddings.

This hymn begins and ends with the picture of God as a king to whom we bring the tribute of our praises, singing—along with the sun, moon, and the angels—eternal "alleluias."

However, in the very center of this text, the image shifts. Instead of a glorious king, Lyte describes God as our infinitely understanding father who knows our "feeble frame": a father who tends, spares, and rescues us, gently bearing us in his hand.

One of my earliest memories is a visit to my grandparents' home in Minnesota. Beside their house was a cornfield, which seemed to me like a thousand-acre farm, but may have been only the neighbor's garden. One day, drawn by curiosity about what was in there, I wandered away from the safety of the backyard. I found out all too soon what was in there: corn, as far as I could see. Disoriented and frightened, because I could see only a patch of blue sky through the green stalks and golden tassels, I did the only thing I could do: I cried at the top of my lungs. Before long—although it seemed like an eternity—my father came, swept me up in his arms, and carried me to safety.

I have other memories of my father's carrying me. When we went to the beach in the summer, he would hoist me onto his shoulders and take me further and further into the crashing breakers. Exhilarated by the juxtaposition of the danger and absolute security, I would splash and play.

I do not remember much about the football games my parents took me to when they could not get a baby-sitter, but I do remember the crowds when the game was over. Sometimes I dared to walk down the stadium aisle myself in the dark shadows of all the tall people, tightly clasping an adult hand. But to be sure of making a safe exit, I much preferred being swung up on to my father's shoulders.

There has been much discussion in recent years about the exclusive use of male language in speaking of God. It is obvious that, since God is neither male nor female, we have, over the years, gotten things out of balance. My heart sings when I hear some of the maternal imagery in trial liturgies and new hymns.

I knew the love of a mother who cared passionately about her children, and I also have been in that role. Even so, I am sure our love did not begin to match God's maternal love. I would agree with the fourteenth-century Julian of Norwich, that "God rejoices that he is our mother."[37]

Because I was once a little girl who often had to be carried in the arms of her strong and protecting father, I'd hate to see us discard the notion that God can be like him, too.

Hymn 448, 449

O love, how deep, how broad, how high

Latin, 15th cent.; tr. Benjamin Webb (1819–1885)

This hymn is a superb example of the texts bequeathed us by the members of the Oxford and Cambridge Camden Movements, who recovered for the church a treasure-trove of medieval texts. Its translator, Benjamin Webb, was a college friend of the great hymnodist, John Mason Neale, with whom he founded the Cambridge Camden Society. After several curacies, Webb was eventually appointed rector of St. Andrew's, Wells Street, London, where the parish gained wide fame for the excellence of its musical services. He wrote widely about ecclesiology and hymnody and translated many ancient texts. For this hymn, Webb selected eight stanzas of a hymn written for the feast of the nativity.

Its style betrays the influence of Thomas à Kempis (1380–1471); in fact, at one time it was thought to be the work of that author. Thomas à Kempis is best known for his classic, *The Imitation of Christ*. His writings are pervaded by a spirit known as *devotio moderna* ("modern devotion"), a term applied to the revival of the spiritual life which, from the end of the fourteenth century, spread from Holland to parts of Germany, France, and Italy. It laid great stress on the inner life of the individual and encouraged methodical meditation, especially on the life and passion of Christ.

Thomas writes, "Let all the study of our heart be, therefore, from henceforth to have our meditation wholly fixed in the life and in the holy teachings of Jesus Christ."[38] This hymn puts that advice into practice by reviewing Jesus' life, from his baptism to his ascension, with the subjective emphasis ("For *us* baptized, for *us* he bore. . . .") typical of *devotio moderna*. These are framed by the introductory and concluding stanzas, which well illustrate Thomas's words: "I shall sing to thee the song of love, and I shall follow Thee, my Beloved, by highness of thought, wheresoever Thou go; and my soul shall never be weary to praise Thee with the joyful song of ghostly love that I shall sing to Thee."[39]

Both tunes chosen for this text express the breadth of that "ghostly love." Hymn 448 sets the text to a strong eighteenth-century French church melody. The music for Hymn 449, contemporary with the text, is believed to have been written in the first quarter of the fifteenth century to commemorate King Henry V's victory over the French at Agincourt.

"How passing thought and fantasy . . . , that God, the Son of God, should take our mortal form for mortals' sake."

"For God so loved the world that he gave his only Son, that whoever believes in him should not perish . . . ." (Jn. 3:16)

We Christians, especially those of us who have listened to the stories of Jesus from childhood, often do not realize what a shocking—even unthinkable—event the Incarnation was. We have, most of us, grown to take it for granted that the Son of God "took mortal form for mortals' sake." It is too easy to sing this hymn without feeling the impact of the scandalous belief that Jesus walked through the events of his life "for us."

We perhaps need to make an imaginary leap, and ask ourselves, "What if we had never heard of him?"

Our small friend Evie never had. She was a child crippled by muscular dystrophy, confined to a wheelchair. Her father, a cantor in a synagogue near our home, also sang in New York City as a freelance baritone in various concert halls and churches. Evie often was taken by her parents to hear him rehearse and perform.

At one point, Evie began talking about what her parents thought was an imaginary friend, a fantasy. She called her friend "the Broken Man." Somehow, the "Broken Man" consoled her about her disability in a way that nothing had before.

One day, the family took Evie to hear her father sing in Riverside Church, the great church that stands on the shore of the Hudson in New York's Morningside Heights. As they were wheeling Evie out of the church, she suddenly became very excited: "There's the Broken Man! There's the Broken Man!"

They followed her gaze. High on the wall was a crucifix. And there, hanging on the crucifix was the Broken Man. He was the first friend Evie had ever found who took her mortal form, so that children like her would know that God cared about brokenness. He was not imaginary, after all.

Evie's parents, pious Jews, did not forget what the Broken Man had given their daughter. Their love for Evie mirrored God's love, so deep, so broad, so high. They gave her a book, *The Greatest Story Ever Told*, with a picture of the crucified Jesus on the bright red cover. And every Christmas they placed a small Christmas tree in the corner of the playroom and framed her bedroom window with colored lights. The Broken Man brought Evie comfort until the day she died, just a few short years later.

Hymn 458

My song is love unknown
Samuel Crossman (1624–1683)

Samuel Crossman was born in Bradfield Monachorum in Suffolk and educated at Pembroke College, Cambridge. Although a Dissenter, he was appointed vicar at All Saints, Sudbury, serving his Anglican congregation and ministering to a Puritan congregation as well. When the Act of Uniformity was imposed in 1662, he was deposed from ministry due to his Puritan leanings. He later conformed, was episcopally ordained, and became one of the King's chaplains. In 1667, he was appointed prebendary of Bristol and vicar of St. Nicholas Church. In 1682, he became treasurer of Bristol Cathedral; he was named dean a year later, just a few weeks before he died.

Upon his death, the cathedral's chancellor wrote: "Mr. Crossman, our new dean, died this morning: a man lamented by few either of the city or neighbourhood. He hath left a debt upon our Church of £300." One cannot help but question why Crossman would have been appointed dean if he had been inept as treasurer, or how a new dean could have accrued such a debt in that short space of time. Can we suspect the motives of the chancellor, who himself had the duty of managing the temporal affairs of the diocese? It is heartening to know that, despite the chancellor's views, Crossman is buried in the cathedral.

This text originally appeared as one of nine poems in Crossman's *The Young Man's Meditations, or some few Sacred Poems upon Selected Subjects, and Scriptures*, published in 1664. The poem is based on Matthew's account of the Passion, with distinct overtones in stanza two of Phil. 2:5–11 and Jn. 1:18, and many other gospel allusions.

The title "love unknown" may derive from George Herbert's allegorical poem by that title, and the fourth line of stanza seven may be an intentional echo of the refrain—"Was ever grief like mine?"—of Herbert's "The Sacrifice." Hymnologist Carl P. Daw, Jr. points out that, like Herbert and the other metaphysical poets, Crossman has adapted to devotional purposes the hyperbolic tone and intensifying techniques associated with Renaissance love poetry. Some of the stylistic devices include wordplay on a common root ("love to the loveless shown, that they might lovely be"); oxymoron ("sweet injuries"); irony ("a murderer they save, the Prince of Life they slay"); claims of uniqueness (in the opening line and in the reiteration of "never"); paradox ("he to suffering goes, that he his foes from thence might free").[40]

Daw comments that these literary devices are applied, for once, to "an event capable of sustaining all this heightened emotion: the suffering of Jesus Christ for the salvation of all humanity."[41]

The music for this text was composed by John Ireland in 1918. The composer was having lunch with Geoffrey Shaw, who handed a slip of paper to Ireland saying, "I want a tune for this lovely poem by Samuel Crossman." The composer took the paper and picked up the menu. After writing on the back of the menu for a few minutes he handed it to Shaw, with the casual remark, "Here is your tune."[42]

"This is my friend." There are many texts about Jesus as our friend, some of them verging on the sentimental, but this one has always moved me most. Its artistry and fervor, expressed in the style of a love poem, fan the flames of ardor.

There are many people who relate to God primarily through friendship with Jesus. Their spirituality is centered on the Lord who walked the earth for thirty-three years in the beginning of our era, and whose resurrected life continues to be a reality for them today.

But there are those who relate to God primarily as the Creator of all that is. There are others who naturally turn in prayer toward the Spirit who pervades all things. Trinitarians believe that each spirituality, while directed toward one Person of the Trinity, is directed to all—the Three in One, the One in Three.

As we grow and mature, we can plunge more and more into the mystery of that Trinity by becoming better acquainted with all three Persons, no matter what our natural inclinations are.

Crossman's hymn speaks to those of us who need to have our ardor for Jesus fanned into a flame. The poet's love song is not about simple-minded coziness or familiarity. Indeed, it is about "love unknown": love beyond our ability to comprehend it. Along with all the great works of art that have managed to portray the earthly Jesus with a sense both of reality and mystery, this hymn conveys a love that transcends the merely sentimental. It touches our hearts with compassion for the man who was the embodiment of love, making the lame to run and the blind to see. We feel the ache in our throats as we sing of his suffering: "Why, what hath my Lord done? / What makes this rage and spite?"

I remember feeling this love for him when I first watched the classic movie *The King of Kings* as a child in elementary school. Watching the actor who played Jesus walking among ordinary human beings, teaching, healing, suffering, dying, and rising, helped me learn to love the original. I still have my sixth-grade diary in which I wrote, on March 18: "Today I went to the movie at the Church House, *The King of Kings*, about the Life of Christ. It showed His life from the time He started to teach. It was the second time I had seen it, but I love it, and I always will."

The love I experienced when I saw *The King of Kings* and feel when I sing this hymn begins not within me, but with "my Savior's love to me." It is Jesus' example of love to the loveless, even his enemies, that touches our hearts. Jesus is the incarnation of God's Passion to heal us and to suffer with us, despite our being undeserving of it. This is, indeed, our friend, in whose sweet praise we all our days could gladly spend.

Hymn 460, 461

Alleluia! sing to Jesus!

William Chatterton Dix (1837–1898)

William Chatterton Dix was the son of a well-known Bristol surgeon and author. He was educated at the Bristol Grammar School, and later became manager of a marine insurance company in Glasgow. A scholarly layman who combined a successful business career with a gift for hymn writing, Dix published several volumes of hymns and devotional works, and rendered a number of Greek and Abyssinian hymns and sequences into metrical form.

"Alleluia! sing to Jesus!" entitled by Dix "Redemption by the Precious Blood," first appeared in Dix's collection *Altar Songs, Verses on the Holy Eucharist* (London, 1867).

Scriptural allusions include Jn.6:32 ("I am the bread of life"); Ps.78:25 ("So mortals ate the bread of angels"); Rev.4:6 ("and in front of the throne there is something like a sea of glass, like crystal"); and Rev.5:9 ("They sing a new song: 'You are worthy to take the scroll and to open its seals, for you were slaughtered and by your blood you ransomed for God saints from every tribe and language and people and nation'").

The hymn conflates the image of monarch ("his the scepter, his the throne") and high priest ("thou within the veil hast entered, robed in flesh, our great High Priest"). The latter image is based on Heb.9:11–14:

> But when Christ came as a high priest of the good things that have come, then through the greater and perfect tent (not made with hands, that is, not of this creation), he entered once for all into the Holy Place, not with the blood of goats and calves, but with his own blood, thus obtaining eternal redemption. For if the blood of goats and bulls, with the sprinkling of the ashes of a heifer, sanctifies those who have been defiled so that their flesh is purified, how much more will the blood of Christ, who through the eternal Spirit offered himself without blemish to God, purify our conscience from dead works to worship the living God!

The writer of Hebrews refers to the Jewish cultic observation of the Day of Atonement. Earlier in

Chapter 9, he refers to a "tent": the portable shrine used in the days before the building of Solomon's temple. This tent had an outer court, the Holy Place, and an inner court, the Holy of Holies, which held the ark of the covenant. On one day of the year, Yom Kippur, the Day of Atonement, the high priest passed through the curtain which normally barred access to the divine presence, to offer the blood of the sacrifices as a propitiation for his own sins and those of his people.

This jubilant hymn is set to the popular Welsh hymn tune HYFRYDOL, which, appropriately, means "joyful," and also to the tune by Samuel Sebastian Wesley written especially for the text.

The priestly imagery in "Alleluia! sing to Jesus!" may be inspired by the Epistle to the Hebrews, but the royal atmosphere is straight out of Dix's Victorian England. Although the monarch's imperial power is a thing of the past, England still cherishes its royal traditions. If you have ever seen the movie of Queen Elizabeth II's coronation, with its pomp and pageantry, you have some idea of what I mean.

Sometimes the church's worship reflects this kind of splendor. I have had occasion to sing this hymn in procession in stately liturgies replete with all the paraphernalia that Anglicans love: music, torches, processional crosses, incense, beautiful vestments. I love walking in processions like this. Although I am basically an introvert, I have enough of the extrovert in me that I love to move down the aisle singing "Alleluia!" to a rousing tune.

But the scholarly and thoughtful Dix sneaks an ambiguous note into the triumphant procession. We sweep down the aisle until we are caught up short by the word at the end of the first stanza: blood. Blood! We continue, however, singing that earth is Jesus' footstool and heaven his throne, until our throat catches again, at the phrase "thou on earth both Priest and Victim." This scepter was gained at a cost.

Contemporary Christians sometimes criticize the use of royal and high priestly imagery for Jesus. Over history, such triumphal symbols may well have contributed their share to the excesses of the church. The church's worldly power may have seemed at one time a thoroughly appropriate reflection of its Lord's royalty. Its ecclesiastical power may have been considered a proper use of its Lord's authority as great High Priest. But because people within the church as well as outside it are all too human, this power has often led to corruption. Those who reject this triumphal imagery prefer to focus, instead, on the cost of Jesus' victory. They emphasize Jesus' servanthood and solidarity with the common people.

Dix's hymn reminds me that one of the glories of the Christian tradition is that we can have it both ways. We can march in glorious processions, and then trade our vestments for aprons in order to feed the victims of hunger in a soup kitchen. We can sing Jesus' praises in churches glowing with the reds, blues, and greens of glorious stained glass, and then stand in silent vigil on the village square for the end of bloodshed around the world. Both are the truth. In both, we celebrate our Lord, who reigns both in the heavenly courts and in the hearts of his most humble brothers and sisters on earth. Alleluia!

Hymn 488

Be thou my vision, O Lord of my heart

Irish, ca. 700, versified Mary Elizabeth Byrne (1880–1931); tr. Eleanor H. Hull (1860–1935)

This prayer from the Irish monastic tradition is an example of a Celtic "lorica" or breastplate, an incantation to be recited for protection.

The Celtic church existed in the British Isles long before the mission of St. Augustine from Rome to Canterbury in 596–597. Its origins are lost in the mists of time, but it is likely that the first Christians to visit Britain and Ireland were probably traders from the Mediterranean; even during the lifetime of Jesus, trade was well established between the Middle East and the British Isles.

With the coming of the Saxons in the fifth century, the Celtic church and its culture almost disappeared, and the Christian communities that survived in Cornwall, Wales, Ireland, and Scotland were cut off from intercourse with Rome and the Continent. It was in part because of that isolation that the Celtic Christians found it difficult to accept the Roman version of Christianity that St.

Augustine brought. They finally submitted in 664 at the Synod of Whitby to the rule of the Roman Church.

Fortunately, the Synod of Whitby was not the last word for Celtic Christianity. It has captured the imagination of present-day Christians and has made a strong impact on contemporary spirituality. Today's Christians who seek to include environmental justice as part of their ethical practice can claim kinship with the Celts, who understood that this world is God's world and that nature and grace are intertwined.

In our present-day search for a spirituality that sanctifies the ordinary moments of our lives, we are learning much from the Celts, who saw the routine tasks of daily life as permeated with the sacred. Moreover, they understood Christ's cross—like the High Crosses in the Irish countryside—as a cross of victory over evil. That idea gives redemptive meaning to humanity's suffering today throughout the world.

We are attracted by the optimism of the Celts. It has been suggested that the very early conversion of the Celtic peoples meant that they received the gospel at a time when the Church emphasized the goodness of God, who healed and restored the whole of human nature, as well as the whole creation.[43]

The Bible was the Celts' main book of study. It is clear that the author of "Be thou my vision" knew Col.1:15–23 ("He is the image of the invisible God. . . ."); Col.2:2–3 (". . . Christ himself, in whom are hidden all the treasures of wisdom and knowledge"); and Gal.2:20 (". . . it is no longer I who live, but it is Christ who lives in me.")

The poem, over a thousand years old, was versified by Mary Elizabeth Byrne, a graduate of the National University of Ireland. She worked from a prose translation by Eleanor H. Hull, the founder and honorary secretary of the Irish Text Society, who was instrumental in promoting a reawakened interest in early Gaelic culture. It is sung to an Irish folk melody named after a hill—*Slane*—associated with Patrick, one of Celtic Christianity's great saints.[44]

What does it mean for Christ to "be our vision"?

In our era, human beings relate to the world—more than at any other time in history—through vision. We get most of our information through looking: at computer screens, books, magazines, newspapers, and the network news. Much of our entertainment is watching: television, sports, movies. Even in the course of one day, we are likely to travel farther away from the familiar sights of home than people have ever done before. The world of advertising utilizes the power of our sense of sight by luring us, through subtle visual suggestion, into a state of dissatisfaction with what we have so that we will buy something we think we want.

We are likely to see, "waking or sleeping," these images which swirl around us. Do you ever find that, even in your dreams, the accumulated images of the day parade in an unending procession through your brain?

What if Christ were our "vision," "our best thought, by day or by night"? And how can we learn that kind of vision?

We do that by looking at the world through new lenses. These lenses are not optical glass; they are "spiritual" lenses. They are not a change of prescription; rather, they are a change of perception. When we put them on, we see, in the light of the "bright heaven's Sun," that the material world is shining with God's presence.

We discover that presence, not merely with our eyes, but with all our senses. In the words of a Celtic prayer:

Bless to me, O God,
Each thing mine eye sees;
Bless to me, O God,
Each sound mine ear hears;
Bless to me, O God,
Each odour that goes to my nostrils;
Bless to me, O God,
Each taste that goes to my lips,
Each note that goes to my song . . . .[45]

The Celts knew that the sacred presence hovered over their daily chores:

> "I will kindle my fire this morning in the presence of the holy angels of heaven . . ."
> "Bless O God my little cow, Bless Thou my partnership and the milking of my hands, O God."
> "Bless, O Chief of generous chiefs,
> My loom and everything a-near me."[46]

Our perception that the holy is not something separate from ordinary life, but embedded in it, helps us "bless" our own daily activities.

Why not go through your day's activities in your mind, and write your own "blessings"? ("I will make my bed this morning in the presence of the holy angels of heaven"; "Bless my hands at this computer, O God".) It just might improve your vision, and certainly would deepen your love of the "Heart of your heart," through whom you see, and in whom you dwell.

Hymn 516

Come down, O Love divine

Bianco da Siena (d.1434?); tr. R. F. Littledale (1833–1890)

Bianco da Siena, born in the middle of the fourteenth century, was trained as a worker in wool. His profession may have earned him his nickname, meaning "white." In 1397 he joined a group first known as *poverelli di Cristo* and later as *Compagnia dei Gesuati*, and lived in their community in Venice. Members of the group were laity who followed the Augustinian Rule and had a great interest in mysticism. The latter caused them to be distrusted by authorities at the Vatican, who feared they might drift into heresy.

Bianco was an ardent poet, who wrote with the intention of strengthening the faith of his brethren. His texts were examples of *laudi*—the extremely popular Italian vernacular hymns of praise and devotion, dating from the time of Francis of Assisi. Congregations called *Companie de Laudesi* or *Laudisti* formed to cultivate this type of devotional singing among the Italian people. It was out of the musical and dramatic representations occurring in their meetings that the oratorio was to develop in the sixteenth century.

In 1851, these hymns were gathered into a collection entitled *Laudi Spirituali*, where they were discovered by English priest and writer R. F. Littledale, a friend of the Pre-Raphaelites, who saw the Middle Ages as a halcyon era for Christianity. Littledale translated this exquisite text for a collection entitled *The People's Hymnal*:

Discendi, amor sante
Visita la mie mente
Del tuo amore ardente,
Si che di te m'infiammi tuto quanto.

Vienne, consolatore,
Nel mio cuor veramente:
Del tuo ardente amore
Ardel veracemente.

Seeing these words out of context, one might expect them to be part of the libretto for a love aria from a dramatic opera. Instead, they are a hymn text, appropriately paired with music by Ralph Vaughan Williams which conveys the soul's breathless desire for God in the urgent rush of the quarter notes that end the second and fourth phrases of each stanza.

Love poetry and the poetry of mysticism can be almost indistinguishable one from the other. Over the centuries, Christian mystics have used erotic images to express their desire for union with the divine. Among these images, the symbol of fire was called upon often to express the threefold mystic journey of purgation (being cleansed of sin), illumination (growing in knowledge and love of God), and union (being united spiritually with God).

To understand the power of that image, we need to imagine the world before the invention of electric lights, when most light, with the exception of the moon, was produced by fire, and all light was hot.

The fire that illuminated darkness and provided warmth also had the capacity to destroy. Its power to purge the impurities in metal is used by Bianco to illustrate his desire to be "consumed" by his ardor for God: *Arda si fortemente Che tuto mi consumi*. (Littledale translated these lines into the more properly Anglican "till earthly passions turn to dust and ashes in its heat consuming.") Bianco prayed to have all that was not of God in him burned away; it was the way he sought his true humanity. It has been said that "anyone who has seen gold being refined knows how beautifully the fire flames up through the gold as it burns the dross and melts the gold. As the gold liquefies, it seems to blossom like a marvelous golden flower." [47]

This is strong language, but does it not express our own most basic longing, when we are quiet enough to think about it, the longing to be united with our Source?

The path of our ordinary lives as Christians is not so far removed from the mystic's path. It begins when love awakens within us, when God becomes to us as real as those more obvious everyday realities which surround us. It continues as love helps us turn from the bondage of selfishness, pride, and greed. Our love makes us take ever greater delight in realizing that God shines through every moment of our daily lives. Along with the illumination that this knowledge gives us, is another illumination: the glow of our hearts, as we give ourselves in service to others.

The mystic way is not reserved for the extraordinary saints of God or for the poets, like Bianco, whose work has survived. The great teacher of prayer, Evelyn Underhill, describes mysticism as "the art of union with Reality."[48] Isn't that what we all want? We find our truest selves when we ardently seek God and become attuned to God's love, so that its fire permeates our life.

Hymn 518,519,520

Christ is made the sure foundation

Latin, ca. 7th cent.

Hymns 518 (*Angularis fundamentum*), 519 and 520, are part of one long hymn of nine stanzas, *Urbs beata Jerusalem,* traditionally associated with the dedication of a church. This ancient text is found in manuscript collections from the ninth century, but perhaps dates from three hundred years earlier.

Since medieval times, the verses have been divided, with Part I (Hymn 519/520) sung at

Vespers and Part II (Hymn 518) sung at Lauds, the Morning Office. John Mason Neale's translation was first included in his *Mediaeval Hymns and Sequences*.

The text is based on 1 Pet. 2:4–5 ("Come to him, a living stone, though rejected by mortals yet chosen and precious in God's sight, and like living stones, let yourselves be built into a spiritual house, to be a holy priesthood, to offer spiritual sacrifices acceptable to God through Jesus Christ."); Eph. 2:19–20 ("So then you are no longer strangers and aliens, but you are citizens with the saints and also members of the household of God, built upon the foundation of the apostles and prophets, with Christ Jesus himself as the cornerstone."); and the vision of the new Jerusalem in Chapter 21 of the Book of Revelation.

The images are a reminder of the words of Jesus in Mt. 7:26–27: "And everyone who hears these words of mine and does not act on them will be like a foolish man who built his house on sand. The rain fell and the floods came, and the winds blew and beat against that house, and it fell—and great was its fall."

The text is matched with the Purcell Tune WESTMINSTER ABBEY. It is known to many Americans through the broadcast of the marriage ceremony of Princess Margaret in 1960, and is often used as a processional hymn at weddings in Episcopal churches.

Unlike passing fads, toys that involve building are never outmoded. Our children had an abundance of building materials: wooden blocks, cardboard "brick blocks," Tinker Toys, Lincoln Logs, Lego. When we went to the beach, sand castles arose. In the woods near our New Hampshire vacation spot, a house of brush from the forest floor soon appeared.

When the children were very young, they would pile block upon block, until we heard the sound of the tower tumbling down on the wood floor, often followed by the sound of either sobs or laughter. They soon became skilled in building a strong foundation and aligning the blocks carefully on top. At the beach, they finally became reconciled to the transitory nature of their carefully contrived stand castles, as the incoming tide devoured them. They loved the story of "The Three Little Pigs," who built houses of straw, sticks, and bricks, and knew that they would have been wise enough to build with the last of the options, should a hungry wolf be in the neighborhood.

We human beings are fascinated with building. Perhaps it is because our skeletons themselves are an architectural construction. The foot with its arches is a Gothic system of stress and counterstress. From that base we are built up: the solid mass of the pelvis centered over our feet, the shoulder joints centered over the hip joints, and the head balanced at the apex of the skeleton.

It is no surprise that architectural images are frequent in the language of religion, for the physical realm and the spiritual realm are often merely different expressions of a common truth.

When we build our lives and our communities, we need a foundation. Such a foundation provides stability of purpose. It keeps us from falling apart like the toppling blocks of a child's tower. Because of the law of gravity, the weight of the entire building is connected to that foundation.

For Christians and their church communities, Jesus Christ is the foundation. Our lives are built on the solid rock of his gospel and his presence with us. He supports us and also connects us.

As part of this living edifice which is the church, we also support one another. I remember visiting Chartres Cathedral and meeting Malcolm Miller, the resident scholar and guide, who gave us a lively demonstration of the principles of Gothic architecture. He asked the six strongest men present to face one another with hands joined, forming a long arch as if they were about to play a game of London Bridge. Then he stooped to walk under the arch and pressed outwards on their bodies, and the arch collapsed.

Next he asked six women to stand behind those men, pressing with their hands against their backs, and repeated the process. This time, because of the strength of the "buttresses," the human cathedral remained intact.

The physics of the Gothic cathedral tells us something about our interior architecture. We need to let our weight sink into our foundation in Christ, through meditation, prayer, and worship. And the same is true for the community of the church, from the smallest rural parish to the entire family of Christendom.

But we also can strengthen our stability through utilizing the physics of gravity, using the support of others who help us direct our weight towards Christ. For the church is a community: not only of those present, but of those past. We are "citizens with the saints and also members of the household of God, built upon the foundation of the apostles and prophets, with Christ Jesus himself as the cornerstone."

Hymn 525

The Church's one foundation

Samuel John Stone (1839–1900)

This hymn was born out of controversy. Samuel John Stone, a curate in Windsor and later known for his work of ministering to the poor in the East End of London, wrote a series of hymns on the Creed. He published these hymns as *Lyra Fidelium: Twelve Hymns on the Twelve Articles of the Apostles' Creed* (1866). The ninth hymn was "The Church's one foundation," headed "Article XI. The Holy Catholic Church: the Communion of Saints. 'He is the Head of the Body, the Church.'"

The church was, in Stone's view, by "heresies distressed." A certain John William Colenso, the Anglican Bishop of Natal in South Africa, had printed some papers on *The Pentateuch and the Book of Joshua Critically Examined* in 1862. One of the early works of Biblical criticism (in the sense of taking seriously the historical, social, and literary context of the Bible), the papers challenged the traditional view of the Scriptures. Colenso's liberal pastoral policies did not help: he did not insist that Africans who came to him for baptism divorce all their wives except one, and was accused of condoning polygamy. Colenso was accused of "doing sums on the Pentateuch" (he had been a teacher of mathematics at Harrow) and undermining the foundations of the Christian faith. He was deposed from his see by Bishop Gray of Cape Town in 1863; and, though he appealed—and won—his case, Gray's defense of tradition inspired many, including Stone. Despite his legal victory, Colenso was excommunicated in 1866. The controversy continued throughout the church, and the result was the first Lambeth Conference in 1867, where the issue was high on the agenda of the bishops who gathered from the worldwide Anglican Communion.

Throughout the rest of the nineteenth century, other controversies were to arise, such as the challenges of Darwinism. Stone's hymn, which spoke to the anxieties of these times, became increasingly popular.

The third Lambeth Conference was held in 1888, and the Lambeth Quadrilateral (the classic Anglican statement regarding the essence of the Christian faith) was adopted. For this historic meeting, a longer ten-stanza version of Stone's hymn, written originally for processional use at Salisbury Cathedral, was sung as the processional hymn at all the three great services at Canterbury Cathedral, Westminster Abbey, and St. Paul's. Afterwards, Bishop Nelson of New Zealand wrote:

Bard of the Church, in these divided days
For words of harmony to thee we praise:
Of love and oneness thou didst strike the chords,
The Church's one Foundation thou didst sing. . . .[49]

The tune by Samuel Sebastian Wesley, grandson of Charles Wesley, was matched with the text in 1868.

It is thought-provoking to read the story of "The Church's one foundation" and to realize how much our outlook has changed since Bishop Colenso's study of the first six books of the Bible shattered the peace of the church. Today, most of us read the Bible like Colenso, rather than like his adversary, Bishop Gray; we find inspiration in recognizing the Spirit's guidance, not merely in the words which are contained between the bindings of our Old and New Testaments, but in the process of how they got there.

One of my New Testament professors was fond of saying "Jesus lived in the era before videotape." The implication of those words is that the history found in the Scripture was seen through human eyes, rather than through a camera. As we know, when five people are asked to describe the same incident, the result is inevitably five different versions of the story, although each version is the truth as understood by the teller. The complexity grows if each person passes on the story to someone else, and the story is told and retold until finally it is written down.

My professor taught me how to apply that lesson to the Gospels. The task became endlessly fascinating; it changed what the Bible meant to me. As I underlined passages, and wrote notes in the margin, something happened: I rediscovered the power in the stories that had become humdrum from over-familiarity. More than that, this study brought me closer to the Jesus who was the subject of so many stories and so much conjecture among his earliest followers.

For me, approaching the Bible as did Bishop Colenso was an experience of "the Church's one foundation is Jesus Christ her Lord"! I am filled with wonder when I observe the Spirit of Christ in shaping what became the Christian Scripture I hold as a book in my hands.

And the story of this hymn also reminds me that, in our controversies, we can never be absolutely certain that we are standing on God's side. Jesus' life was not recorded on videotape. Nor do we hear present truth from God's loudspeaker. The best we can do is to listen to one another in humility. We may think we are basing our opinions on the foundation of Jesus Christ, but perhaps, instead, we are blocking the work of the Spirit. We can never know, in this life.

Meanwhile, underneath all of us is the Foundation on which we stand—the Lord Jesus who probably smiles at our petty quarrels and eagerly waits for us to enter the church triumphant in eternity.

Hymn 541

Come, labor on

Jane Laurie Borthwick (1813–1897)

Jane Laurie Borthwick, the descendant of an old Scottish family, was the daughter of the manager of the North British Insurance Office in Edinburgh. Following a trip to the continent, her father encouraged Jane and her sister Sarah to translate German hymns. The result was *Hymns from the Land of Luther*, which included four volumes published between 1854 and 1862. They contained one hundred twenty-two hymns, sixty-one by Jane and fifty-three by Sarah. It was not long before many of these translations were printed in other hymnals, both in England and in America.

Borthwick appropriated the initials H.L.L. from the title of the book and used them as a pseudonym for many of her hymns that appeared in two subsequent volumes, *Family Treasury* and *Thoughts for Thoughtful Hours*. A collection of translations of poems by the German poet Meta Heusser-Schweitzer was published in 1875 under the title of *Alpine Lyrics*.

A devoted member of the Free Church of Scotland, Borthwick was active in various religious and social causes.

"Come, labor on" was written by Borthwick for her *Thoughts for Thoughtful Hours* (1859). Using New Testament imagery, this hymn for church-workers likens the winning of souls to the harvesting of grain.

A stirring tune by T. Tertius Noble mirrors the vigor of the text.

I have to admit that, at an earlier period in my life, singing this hymn exhausted me. "Come, labor on" was not the kind of thing I wanted to hear after a long week; I would have preferred a hymn about resting in Jesus' presence.

But I have learned better. I have learned that one of the great blessings of life is the opportunity to do meaningful work. When we labor at something we like to do, with the purpose of enhancing the well-being of the world, we are doing the work of God, whether or not we are the church-workers for which this hymn was written.

When I was young, I was always puzzled about the work my father did each day when he left in the morning to commute to New York City. I knew he looked like the other businessmen on the train, and, since I was much more impressed by people who were in the arts, I am sure I undervalued his work. I knew little about what he actually did as a management consultant and career counselor until after he died, when letters to my mother poured into our home. "Your husband changed my life; he directed me in the right direction toward a career which has been deeply satisfying." "His advice kept me sane." "He helped our chaotic company work again."

My father, I learned, had done God's work in a way I had never fully realized. He had an intuitive sense of the gifts of other people and could guide them towards appropriate career paths. When it came to management consulting, he was a kind of healer, first diagnosing what was wrong in struggling organizations and then prescribing a cure. As a result, he was a much loved colleague and mentor, worthy indeed of the welcome "Servant, well done."

Frederich Beuchner writes about vocation:

> There are all different kinds of voices calling you to all different kinds of work, and the problem is to find out which is the voice of God rather than of Society, say, or the Super-ego, or Self-Interest.
>
> By and large a good rule for finding out is this. The kind of work God usually calls you to is the kind of work (a) that you need most to do and (b) that the world most needs to have done. . . .
>
> The place God calls you to is the place where your deep gladness and the world's deep hunger meet.[50]

The place of our deep gladness and the world's deep hunger. That is what makes labor sacred, whether it be the unsung labor of a parent caring for a child, the faithful labor of those who care for our houses and highways so that we will be secure and safe, the patient labor of the farmer or counselor, the creative labor of the artist or musician, or the skilled labor of the surgeon or physicist. All work, in their own ways, at tending the world God created, if it is a labor of love. "Servants, well done."

Hymn 544

Jesus shall reign where'er the sun

Isaac Watts (1674–1748)

Born in Southampton, England, Isaac Watts is often called the father of English hymnody. He displayed the symptoms of his vocation at a very early age. The story goes that he had an annoying habit of rhyming even everyday conversation; one day, when he was scolded by his irritated father for this practice, he cried out, "O, Father, do some pity take, and I will no more verses make."

Despite poor health, he was to become a scholar in many different fields. His works, among which were essays, discussions of psychology, sermons, catechisms, theological treatises, and textbooks on logic, wielded a powerful influence upon the thinking of the late seventeenth and early eighteenth centuries. His poetic gifts were such as to prompt Samuel Johnson to include Watts in his *Lives of the Poets*. His lasting fame, however, eventually rested on his hymns and paraphrases. When he died, a monument honoring him was placed in Westminster Abbey.

It is interesting to note that, more than sixty years after the publication of this hymn in 1719, there were still Christians who believed that no hymns other than metrical psalms were proper for worship. An incident in Elizabeth, New Jersey, in May 1780, during the American Revolution is proof. George Washington's militia ran out of wadding for their guns, and the local Presbyterian pastor, obviously of the "metrical hymn school," used the opportunity to bring out batches of Watts's hymns, shouting "Give 'em Watts, boys; give 'em Watts!"

Nine years later, during the first General Assembly of the Presbyterian Church in Philadelphia, a clergyman rode on horseback from his Kentucky parish to plead with the assembly to refuse to allow the pernicious error of adopting the use of Watts's hymns in public worship; the assembly, however, requested him to use Christian charity toward those who differed from him in their views. One wonders what these early dissidents would think of the inclusion of eleven of Watts's hymn texts in the 1990 Presbyterian hymnal, to say nothing of sixteen texts in *The Hymnal 1982*!

This hymn is often referred to as the first great missionary hymn written in English. Entitled "Christ's Kingdom among the Gentiles," it was first published in Watts's *Psalms of David*, 1719. A free paraphrase of Psalm 72, a prayer for God's blessing upon the son of a Hebrew king, the hymn is an example of the way Watts "Christianized" the Psalms.

It is interesting to note that, when this hymn was written, the great missionary movement had scarcely begun; it was not until the last quarter of the eighteenth century that the Protestant Church felt an obligation to spread the gospel to other lands. Even at that late date, an Anglican bishop made the contemptuous remark to an enthusiastic missionary, "Young man, if God wants to save the heathen, He will do it without any help from you."[51]

The text is matched with an eighteenth-century psalm tune.

Isaac Watts, in writing this hymn, holds before us the vision of a Christian "empire," in which people and realms of every tongue worship Jesus. In two stanzas omitted in most recent hymnals, the non-Christian world is pictured as exotic and distant: "Behold the islands with their kings / And Europe her best tribute brings; / From North to South the princes meet / To pay their homage at his feet. / There Persia, glorious to behold / There India shines in Eastern gold; / And barbarous nations at his word / Submit, and bow, and own their Lord."

England's empire was still intact during Isaac Watts's life, so this vision of universal Christianity was not as improbable as it seems to us today. Although missionaries did indeed travel to the far corners of the globe to preach the gospel, Watts would be surprised to learn that, more than two hundred and fifty years after his death, barely a third of the world's population would call themselves Christian.

While courageous men and women continue to bring the good news, as well as practical manifestations of its message of healing and compassion, all over the world, it is heartening to think that there are also other, more subtle ways to spread the gospel throughout the world.

Our world grows ever smaller, as we move towards a global economy. Intercontinental travel is almost as easy today as a day's ramble into the next county would have been for Isaac Watts. The Eastern gold of India and the glories of Persia are little more than a day's journey away for most of us. All countries, from the most powerful to the most impoverished, are inextricably intertwined, through travel, communication, commerce, and finance.

This interconnection provides us with an opportunity: we can spread the good news through our behavior towards these no longer distant neighbors of ours. We may not name our actions the "gospel of Jesus Christ," but we are helping Jesus' reign to become universal through our respect, concern, and compassion.

There are many ways we can bring our faith to bear on decisions about the way people of other countries and cultures are treated. When we write to our governmental leaders urging them to continue to negotiate before using force in international conflicts, we are preaching Jesus' message of peace. When we hold our corporations accountable for making enormous profits through the use of underpaid labor in developing countries, we are proclaiming the gospel of justice. When we provide shelter for exiles, or help them build their own homes, we are helping the weary to find rest. When we send medicine and food to the "sons of want" struggling for survival in the midst of war or natural disasters, we are practicing mercy. When we write letters urging foreign leaders to free so-called "dissidents" from prison, we are helping the prisoners lose their chains.

Sadly, many of the global sins against the gospel, from religious wars to corporate greed, are perpetrated by people who call themselves Christians. It is up to all of us to confront these sins. In this day, it is those who practice the gospel—whether they call themselves Christians or not—who contribute to the vision of Isaac Watts. Although we may not name what we do as missionary work, that is what we are doing: spreading the good news to people and realms of every tongue.

Hymn 546

Awake, my soul, stretch every nerve

Philip Doddridge (1702–1751)

Doddridge was born in London, the youngest of twenty children of a London merchant, eighteen of whom had died in infancy. He was orphaned at an early age, and the Duchess of Bedford offered to send him to Cambridge. Because the offer contained the obligation to become an Anglican priest, he enrolled instead at the nonconformist academy in Kibworth and became minister of Kibworth chapel in 1723. While there, he discovered the tremendous usefulness of hymns as an aid in preaching the gospel to his humble parish: "poor men in smock frocks and hobnail boots, and poor women in cloaks and pattens. . . . I have not so much as a tea-table in my whole diocese, and but one hoop petticoat."[52]

While at Kibworth, he consulted with Isaac Watts about the founding of a nonconformist academy in the Midlands, and a friendship began which was to continue until Watts's death. In 1729, Doddrige was called to Chapel Hill Congregational Church in Northampton, where he founded his own academy, which would ultimately train two hundred young men for the ministry. It was observed that he never wasted a minute; even while he was shaving and dressing, he had a student read to him. In 1736 he received the D.D. degree from the University of Aberdeen.

A man of great learning and writer of many theological works, Doddridge was the first nonconformist leader to show any sympathy for the work of the two great evangelists who were responsible for the religious awakening of the eighteenth century, Whitefield and Wesley. He was known and respected not only by fellow independents such as Watts, but by Anglicans such as Bishops William Warburton and Thomas Seeker.

Doddridge fought tuberculosis for years. When Lady Huntingdon, one of Whitefield's financial backers, made it possible for him to take a voyage to Lisbon for his health, he said to her in parting, "I can as well go to heaven from Lisbon as from my own study at Northampton."[53] He died in Lisbon and is buried there in the English cemetery near the novelist Henry Fielding. All of his four hundred hymns were published posthumously in 1755 by his friend Job Orton.

While Doddridge wrote in the style of Watts, his hymns reflect a greater awareness of the social message of the gospel than those of his colleague. They reveal some of the earliest missionary zeal in hymnody, anticipating by more than a half century the missionary movement of the early nineteenth century.

This hymn, given the title "Pressing on in the Christian Race," was written to be sung following one of Doddridge's sermons. It is based on Phil. 3:12–14:

> Not that I have already obtained this or have already reached the goal; but I press on to make it my own, because Christ Jesus has made me his own. Beloved, I do not consider that I have made it my own; but this one thing I do: forgetting what lies behind and straining forward to what lies ahead, I press on towards the goal for the prize of the heavenly call of God in Christ Jesus.

There are echoes also of 1 Cor. 9:24 ("Do you not know that in a race the runners all compete, but only one receives the prize? Run in such a way that you may win it."); Heb.12:1 (". . . let us run with perseverance the race that is set before us"), and 2 Tim. 4:8 ("From now on there is reserved for me the crown of righteousness. . . ."). Dr. Charles S. Robinson, New York Presbyterian minister in the late nineteenth century, commented that the hymn is a "matchless challenge—ringing like a trumpeter's note to start the athletes."[54]

The text is matched with a vigorous Handel tune, whose dotted rhythms contribute to the hymn an athletic vitality.

Even as an adult I do not like to be sedentary. Interminable meetings and long car trips are physical torture for me, and, when I am writing, I usually break away from the computer in the middle of the day for a spin on the nearby bike path or a swim at the gym. So you can imagine my constant activity as a child, always moving, running, jumping, climbing, and playing. I loved the activities in gym class and on the playground at recess.

When I came to Sunday school in patent leather shoes and my best dress, I sat quietly during the children's worship service. But how I loved standing up to sing this hymn! "Awake, my soul, stretch every nerve." This hymn and its companion in my personal hit parade, "Stand up, stand up, for Jesus," were about being fully, vibrantly alive. I would sing them with all the strength of my small voice, breathing in new oxygen and letting "every nerve"—and muscle—stretch.

Even as a child, I would have understood Paul's athletic metaphor for Christian living: "Do you not know that in a race all the runners compete, but only one receives the prize? Run in such a way that you may win it." (1 Cor. 9:24) In a race, it is not only the person who crosses the finish line first who has run with the desire to win. I understood that. In our annual elementary school "field day," when I took part in races, there was no question about doing so halfheartedly. I ran with zeal. No wonder this hymn spoke to me.

This text, even now, "recharges" my energy to live as a Christian. It reminds me that the spiritual life has some of the characteristics of aerobic exercise. Such exercise keeps us healthy by challenging us. Aerobic exercise—whether it be running, swimming, dancing, cross-country skiing, or cycling—increases the heart rate over a long enough period of time that both the heart and the lungs become stronger. When I do those things, I have the distinct impression that my lungs have actually expanded so that there is a larger space inside my chest than before. The energy it generates is tangible: when I have been cross-country skiing in the bitter cold, it feels as if there is a small furnace burning warmly inside my ribcage.

Sometimes our spiritual lives feel like a small drowsy child in Sunday school, and our faith seems to be slumbering. A crisis might suddenly "awake our souls," causing us to turn desperately towards God.

But there is a better way to keep our souls awake. We can be like the athlete who prepares for the race through regular training. Over the days and weeks and years, we can increase our capacity to breathe the oxygen of prayer, until our zeal is habitual. Whatever our age, we can then stretch every nerve and press on with vigor, towards the immortal crown that God wants to award every one of us.

Hymn 564,565

He who would valiant be

Percy Dearmer (1867–1936), after John Bunyan (1628–1688)

John Bunyan was born in Elstow, England, the son of a tinker. He learned reading and writing at the village school, took up his father's trade, and was drafted into the Parliamentary Army. He became an avid student of Scripture and, in 1653, joined a Nonconformist (Baptist) church in Bedford. He was soon inspired with the resolve to become a preacher so that "he might mend the souls of people as well as their pots and pans."[55]

During the Restoration, Bunyan was arrested for preaching in a "conventicle," or illegal meeting. When promised pardon if he would stop preaching, he replied, "If I were out of prison today, I would preach the gospel again tomorrow, by the help of God."[56] He spent most of the next twelve years in Bedford gaol. He wrote nine books during the first half of this period. The principal work was *Grace Abounding to the Chief of Sinners*, which was soon followed by *A Confession of my Faith, and a Reason of my Practice*, a spiritual biography.

Released by the Declaration of Indulgence of Charles II in 1672, he was called as pastor to the Bedford church, which met in a barn. From there, he preached throughout the shire so effectively that he was dubbed "Bishop Bunyan."

When Parliament revoked the Declaration of Indulgence, Bunyan lost his license to preach, but he persisted and was soon jailed again. The original warrant for his arrest reads:

> yett once John Bunnyon of your said Towne, Tynker, hath divers times within one month last past in contempt of his Majestie's good

> laws preached or teached at a Conventicle meeteing or assembly under colour or pretense of exercise of Religion in other manner the Church of England.[57]

During this period in jail, he is thought to have finished the first part of *The Pilgrim's Progress,* which he had begun during his first imprisonment. The first part of the book was published in 1678, and the completed work was published in 1685.

The Pilgrim's Progress is an allegory which takes the form of a dream by the author: "As I walk'd through the wilderness of this world, I lighted on a certain place where there was a Den, and I laid me down in that place to sleep; and as I slept, I dreamed a Dream."[58] (It is likely that the "Den" refers to the tiny gate-house prison half way across the narrow bridge that spanned the river Ouse in Bedford.)

The book is the story of Christian, who flees from the City of Destruction and travels as a pilgrim through such landscapes as the Slough of Despond, the Valley of Humiliation, the Vanity Fair, Doubting Castle, and the Delectable Mountains, until he finally reaches the Celestial City.

Part II tells the story of Christian's wife, Christiana, who sets out on the same pilgrimage, accompanied by her neighbor Mercy, despite the objections of Mrs. Timorous and others.

The work, remarkable for the beauty and simplicity of its language, the vividness of its characterization, and the author's sense of humor and feeling for the world of nature, was circulated at first primarily in uneducated circles. Universal in its appeal, it has been translated into well over one hundred languages.

Included in *Pilgrim's Progress* are numerous poems reflecting upon the prose narrative. The poem which became our hymn appeared first in the 1684 edition. It follows and reinforces Valiant-for-Truth's account of his parents and friends who tried to discourage his being a pilgrim:

Who would true Valour See,
Let him come hither;
One here will Constant be,
Come Wind, come Weather.
There's no Discouragement,
Shall make him once Relent,
His first avow'd Intent,
To be a Pilgrim.

Who so beset him round
With dismal Storys,

Do but themselves confound;
His strength the more is,
No Lyon can him fright,
He'll with a Gyant Fight,
But he will have a right,
To be a Pilgrim.
Hobgoblin, nor foul Fiend,
Can daunt his Spirit:
He knows, he at the end,
Shall Life Inherit.
Then Fancies fly away,
He'll fear not what men say,
He'll labor Night and Day,
To be a Pilgrim.[59]

The poem was adapted by Percy Dearmer, an English priest and social activist who was one of seven scholars of the "High Church Party" who decided to compile a hymnal that might become "a humble companion to the Book of Common Prayer."[60] The result was *The English Hymnal*, published in London in 1906. Its musical editors were Ralph Vaughan Williams and Martin Shaw, Dearmer's organist at St. Mary the Virgin, Primrose Hill. The book included texts by the English writers Heber, Keble, Christopher Wordsworth, Cowper, Doddridge, Watts, translations from Latin and Greek by John Mason Neale and from German by Catherine Winkworth and Robert Bridges, and American texts which included works by Whittier, Bryant, Holmes, Lowell, and George W. Doane. Dearmer later wrote:

> In 1904, we who were working at the *English Hymnal* felt that some cheerful and manly hymns must be added to the usual repertory; and this song sprang to my mind. It was a daring thing to add the song to a hymn-book, and it had never been attempted before. To include the hobgoblins would have been to ensure disaster; to ask the congregation of St. Ignotus, Erewhon Park, to invite all to come and look at them, if they wished to see true valor would have been difficult. But when, with the help of the marvelous folk-tune which Vaughan Williams had discovered, we had made a great hymn, it became easy for our imitators to complain that we had altered the words. We felt that we had done rightly; and that no one would have been more distressed than Bunyan himself to have people singing about hobgoblins in church. He had not written it for a hymn, and it was not suitable as a hymn without adaptation.[61]

Bunyan's text was set to music by Winfrid Douglas, while on the train between New York City and Peekskill, where he resided on the grounds of the Community of St. Mary in a stone house named "St. Dunstan's Cottage."

H.R. Haweis, in his foreword to an 1898 edition of *The Pilgrim's Progress*, suggests that Bunyan's great work

> . . . did for Protestantism what Dante did for Roman Catholicism—whilst exposing some times naively its weak points, it affirmed its doctrines, and popularized their application to current life. . . . Bunyan supplied that imaginative touch and that glow of pictorial sentiment without which no religious message seems to win the masses.[62]

Like Jesus, who did not teach the people "without a parable" (Mt.13:32), both Bunyan and Dante were able to capture the essence of religion through a rousing good story. John Dominic Crossan's fascinating book *In Parables* includes some comments about why such stories wield their power. He quotes Ezra Pound:

> In writing poems, the author must use his image because he sees it or feels it, not because he thinks he can use it to back up some creed. All poetic language is the language of exploration. . . . The image is itself the speech. The image is the word beyond formulated language.[63]

In Bunyan's tale, as in Dante's *Commedia* and the parables of Jesus, the story can stand on its own. We do not need to interpret it in order to enjoy it.

Nevertheless, the story works on us, usually unnoticed, at an unconscious level. The fact is that the narratives we read—or, in this day, watch—begin to shape the way we think about the world. Recently, a six-year-old boy shot and killed a classmate because the stories he imbibed from violent television programs shaped the way he thought, before he was old enough to understand the consequences of violence in "real life."

When I was in elementary school, my favorite book was Louisa May Alcott's *Little Women*, the story of the close-knit March family, written in the mid-nineteenth century. I used to read and re-read it, each time trying to decide which of the four sisters—Meg, Jo, Beth, or Amy—I liked best. Because I lived and breathed that story so often, the story began to shape me. Imagine my surprise when I opened my yellowed childhood copy to discover the Preface:

> Go then, my little Book, and show to all
> That entertain and bid thee welcome shall,
> What thou dost keep close shut up in
>   thy breast;
> And wish what thou dost show them to
>   be blest
> To them for good, may make them choose
>   to be
> Pilgrims better, by far, than thee or me.
> Tell them of Mercy; she is one
> Who early hath her pilgrimage begun.
> Yet, let young damsels learn of her to prize
> The world which is to come, and so be wise;
> For little tripping maids may follow God
> Along the ways which saintly feet have trod.
>
> Adapted from John Bunyan[64]

John Bunyan himself knew the power of narrative to inspire or dishearten us. One of the dangers that his pilgrim Christian encountered was the encounter with those "who so beset him round / with dismal stories." That obstacle to the journey was overcome only by Christian's vow "to be a pilgrim."

What stories have shaped each of us through life? In my own, *Little Women* soon had companions: Dante, the Bible, and biographies of people I admire. These narratives, which have almost become a part of my nervous system, inspire and encourage me. They remind me that my own life is a narrative in the making, and that my path, perhaps, might someday influence others. They help me to labor, night and day, to be a pilgrim.

Hymn 594, 595

God of grace and God of glory
Harry Emerson Fosdick (1878–1969)

Harry Emerson Fosdick was born in Buffalo, New York, received a B.A. from Colgate University, a B.Div. from Union Theological Seminary, and a M.A. from Columbia University. He was ordained as a Baptist minister in 1903, served as pastor in the First Baptist Church in Montclair, New Jersey, and was appointed professor of practical theology at Union Seminary in 1915. During World War I, he spent six months visiting soldiers overseas under the auspices of the YMCA and the British Ministry of Information. While at Union, he became a regular "guest preacher" at the First Presbyterian Church in New York until fundamentalist pressure caused him to be expelled from its pulpit because of his liberal views. At this point, John D. Rockefeller invited him to become the pastor of the Park Avenue Baptist Church. At first, Fosdick declined, commenting that Mr. Rockefeller was "too wealthy," to which Rockefeller replied, "Do you think more people will criticize you on account of my wealth than will criticize me on account of your heresy?" Fosdick finally decided to accept, laying down certain conditions, including the provision that a new church be built in "a less swank district."

Soon thereafter Riverside Church was built on Morningside Heights, providing a wide and interdenominational ministry for Fosdick. From its pulpit, he preached to enormous congregations and reached millions of others by means of his more than thirty-two books and his "National Vespers" radio broadcasts. An early supporter of pastoral counselling and of the church's cooperation with psychiatry, he became one of the most influential twentieth-century interpreters of religious belief and thought in America.

His popular hymn "God of grace and God of glory" was written at Fosdick's summer home at Boothbay Harbor, Maine. It was sung for the opening service of Riverside Church on October 5, 1930, and again at the dedication service on February 8, 1931. The text inspired the title of Fosdick's autobiography *The Living of These Days* (1956).

Fosdick conceived of the text as being sung to the tune *Regent Square* and was not happy when it soon was sung to other tunes. In *The Hymnal 1982*, the two choices are a Welsh tune with which the text is ecumenically associated and a tune, by a nineteenth century American composer, first paired with the text in *The Hymnal 1940*.

When we meditate on the evil in the world, it is tempting to believe that one person can do nothing to change things. To avoid "weak resignation," we need reminders from people like the admissions officer of my college who created a poster with the motto: "Think one person can change the world? So do we." Since I have come back to live in the town where that college is located, I have become friends with many students. I admire their energetic idealism—sometimes to the point of contentiousness—and their willingness to put themselves on the line for justice. I fervently hope that they are typical of the young people about to be launched into the world from all our institutions of higher learning.

Harry Emerson Fosdick would have fit right in here. He preached a "social Gospel" from the pulpit at Riverside Church: the "good news" that the Christian ought to change the world. This was no easy optimism; change is always hard-won, and the church would need wisdom and courage in its struggle against the hosts of evil. Her people would first need to be transformed themselves: from proud and selfish people, "rich in things and poor in soul," to brave, informed warriors of peace.

Those of us within the church often underestimate the power we have in the eyes of the world. But it is a reality that was brought home to me recently through an interesting sequence of events. I had become concerned about a proposal for a cargo jetport in our rural county that would destroy the quality of life for those who lived nearby; it was an issue both of social justice and of environmental stewardship. I wrote to the county commissioner and got a prompt telephone call inviting me to come to meet with him, with any friends I would like to bring along.

It was only when I issued the first invitation to a friend, and he looked at me with disbelief, that I found out how extraordinary the commissioner's response to me had been. My friend, a public official himself, had been trying to get the commissioner's ear for weeks about the same issue, but had failed. As we discussed the mystery of why the commissioner had responded to me so promptly, we both realized that perhaps it was because he had spied "The Rev." at the top of my stationery.

My friends and I did meet with the commissioner, and a "town meeting" was planned, to which over 150 upset people came. Before our meeting, the commissioner had heard only those special interest groups who hoped to gain financially from the proposed plan. But now the commissioner heard the voices of his constituents, and we are hoping that the issue is a dead one.

One little letter with "The Rev." at the top! It made me realize that the church has power, and we might as well use that power for God's purposes. Think one Christian can change the world? I think so! For that person represents something greater: the power on earth of the church community, strengthened by the eternal power of God.

Hymn 618

Ye watchers and ye holy ones

John Athelstan Laurie Riley (1858–1945)

John Riley was born in London and educated at Eton and at Pembroke College, Oxford. He traveled extensively in Persia, Turkey, and Kurdistan. This experience provided material for several pamphlets and articles on Greek Orthodox, Nestorian, and other Eastern Christian churches, as well as material for his book *Athos, or the Mountain of Monks* (1887). He published a revision of the Prayer Book, and wrote *The Religious Question in Public Education* (1911) and *Concerning Hymn Tunes and Sequences* (1915).

Riley was one of the leading figures in the preparation of the *English Hymnal* (1906) edited by Percy Dearmer and Ralph Vaughan Williams, and contributed seven translations of Latin hymns and three of his own compositions to this work. The collection, "offered as a humble companion to the Book of Common Prayer for use in the Church" was a pioneer among twentieth-century hymnals in recovering the great classic hymnody of earlier centuries, reawakening an interest in authentic folk music, and introducing new hymns and tunes by modern authors and composers. It set a standard of editorial excellence that greatly influenced later hymnals.

A member of the House of Laymen of the Province of Canterbury for most of his life, Riley was an ardent supporter of the Anglo-Catholic movement. He was living on the Island of Jersey when it was invaded by the Germans during World War II, and died there on November 17, 1945.

This antiphonal song of praise reflects the author's interest in the Eastern church. Stanza one mentions the nine orders of angels codified by the Pseudo-Dionysius, a mystical theologian who lived around 500. Stanza two is a direct paraphrase of the *Theotokion*, the "Hymn to the Mother of God" sung in the early Greek church at the close of every choir office. Stanza three calls upon the departed saints, patriarchs, prophets, apostles and martyrs, while stanza four is an invitation to the saints on earth to join the song of praise.

The tune was arranged by Ralph Vaughan Williams for use with this text in the *English Hymnal*.

Angels are "in." Cherubs peek out from behind the postmarks on "Love" postage stamps, and archangels in all their Florentine glory adorn the covers of coffee table books. In our culture's ambivalent flirtation with the supernatural, angels have become a safe borderland territory, the region where the desire for celestial protection can be satisfied. The popular idea of the function of angels is typified by the small card once given me by a hospice nurse, in which a radiant winged being hovers over two children crossing a bridge, presumably guiding them safely on the passage between life and death.

No matter how sentimentalized it may be, our society's fascination with heavenly beings is, in part, a good sign, leading us gently towards an acknowledgment that there is something beyond what our human senses can perceive.

I remember being part of a discussion on the elementary school playground among several skeptical six-year-olds who were discussing the relative reality of Santa Claus, fairies, elves, the Easter Bunny, and angels. I am less convinced about the first part of the list than I was as an imaginative child, but I have become ever more convinced of the presence of unseen spirits who are messengers of God.

It is not a New Age idea at all. Angels appear in Genesis, Daniel, Isaiah, and Revelation. Angels take part in some of the most important events in the Gospels, announcing Jesus' conception and birth, ministering to him in the desert, strengthening him during his agony in the garden of Gethsemane, and becoming the first witnesses of his Resurrection. Jesus himself taught that the angels are spiritual beings (Mt. 22:30) who always enjoy the face of God in heaven (Mt. 18:10) and would accompany him at his second coming (Mt. 16:17).

Where are angels today? The author Frederick Buechner writes,

> Sleight-of-hand magic is based on the demonstrable fact that as a rule people see only what they expect to see. Angels are powerful spirits whom God sends into the world to wish us well. Since we don't expect to see them, we don't. An angel spreads his glittering wings over us, and we say things like "It was one of those days that made you feel good just to be alive" or "I had a hunch everything was going to turn out all right" or "I don't know where I ever found the courage."[65]

It makes perfect sense to me that there is a sacred order of beings whose purpose is to reflect God's goodness into the world. In the words of the early medieval theologian Pseudo-Dionysius,

> The goal of a hierarchy [of angels], then, is to enable beings to be as like as possible to God and to be at one with him . . . [Angels] are images of God in all respects, . . . clear and spotless mirrors reflecting the glow of primordial light and indeed of God himself. . . . [When they] have received this full and divine splendor they can then pass on this light generously and in accordance with God's will to beings further down the scale.[66]

It also makes perfect sense that, when we worship God, we are joining the ongoing praises of the heavenly courts. Therefore, with Angels and Archangels ("bright seraphs, cherubim, and thrones . . . / dominions, princedoms, powers, / virtues, archangels, angels' choirs"), and with all the company of heaven, we raise the glad strain, Alleluia!

Hymn 645,646

The King of love my shepherd is
Henry Williams Baker (1821–1877)

Born at Belmont House in Vauxhall, London, Baker was the eldest son of Admiral Henry Loraine Baker, a baronet. He was educated at Trinity College, Cambridge, and named vicar of Monkland, near Leominster, in 1844. He succeeded to the baronetcy in 1859, but remained at Monkland until his death.

Baker was a high churchman, who advocated the celibacy of the clergy and produced two devotional books for his parish: *Family Prayers for the Use of those who have to work hard* and a *Daily Text Book*. Baker made a large contribution to the important hymn collection *Hymns Ancient and Modern*, published in London in 1861. As editor, he was prone to making changes in the submitted texts, which led one contributor to quip that *HA&M* should stand for "Hymns Asked for and Mutilated."[67] He also translated Latin hymns, wrote original texts, composed tunes, and engaged the services of other fine hymnwriters, including Monk, Dykes, Elvey, Stainer, and Barnby.

"The King of love my shepherd is," one of the most beloved of hymns, is, like many of the hymns of Luther and Watts, a "Christianized" psalm. The "cup" of Psalm 23 becomes a eucharistic chalice and the cross takes its place with the rod and the staff. The shepherd of the psalm becomes the Good Shepherd of John's gospel (Jn.10:11–18).

John Ellerton wrote in *Church Hymns*, published in London in 1874:

> It may interest many to know that the third verse ["Perverse and foolish oft I strayed"] of this lovely hymn, perhaps the most beautiful of all the countless version of Psalm xxiii, was the last audible sentence upon the dying lips of the lamented author. February 12, 1877.[68]

The text is matched to two equally loved tunes, an Irish melody and the tune composed at Baker's request for the appendix of *Hymns Ancient and Modern*.

—

When I lead workshops in movement as prayer, I almost always use Psalm 23 as a text for interpretation. I usually divide the group into small subgroups, giving each either a verse of the psalm or a stanza of this hymn. The group's task is to meditate upon the text and then to decide how they will express the words without speaking—in "body language."

This may seem like a game of pious charades, but it is far from that: it is prayer. All language has its origin in a non-verbal part of our brain, what scientists call the "right hemisphere." Religious language, in particular, has its origins in that part of our brain where we "know" but cannot yet express what we know through language, a function of the left hemisphere.

Therefore, expressing Psalm 23 without our usual dependence upon speech can take us into the very origin of thought. This psalm, probably first sung by a king who knew well what it was to be the guardian of a flock of sheep, is based on the experience of God as a shepherd. His experience gave rise to a theological intuition which finally became poetry.

Now that David's poem is the most popular psalm in the Hebrew Scriptures, how can we recapture this text's experiential quality, its freshness and depth?

In my workshops, the groups gather after a period of time to "pray" their portion of the psalm in the presence of one another. Each time this happens, no matter what the setting or group, Psalm 23 comes alive in a different way.

I once introduced this exercise to a monastic community which included a quite elderly monk who depended on a cane for walking. He immediately rallied his younger brethren, got them down on all fours, and prodded them with his cane, as he nudged them towards "green pastures." That image of the wise yet persistent guidance of an elder remains with me, as a picture of one of the ways we learn to serve God through the length of our days.

I have memories of two women "spreading a table" with careful and attentive hospitality, of two members of a group tenderly anointing one another's foreheads in a healing gesture, and of two men cowering in fear as they traverse "death's dark vale" until a third lays a hand on their shoulders. I no longer just hear this psalm: I see it.

In these workshops, all of us in attendance, whether participants or observers, make a dual journey. One of them is a journey back in time to the origins of the theology ultimately expressed in the poetry. The second is a journey inward, to the hidden place where we ourselves discover anew—and experience with mind, heart, and body—that the Lord God of the psalmist David is our king of love as well.

Hymn 661

They cast their nets in Galilee
William A. Percy (1885–1942)

William Percy was born in Greenville, Mississippi, the son of LeRoy Percy, a United States senator from Mississippi. After earning a Bachelor of Laws degree from Harvard University, he practiced law with his father in Greenville until World War I broke out. Percy served overseas, distinguishing himself in work for the Belgian Relief during 1916 and 1917 and then as a captain of the 37th Division for the next two years. He received the Croix de Guerre with gold and silver stars.

Percy returned to Greenville after the war and settled on the family estate, Trail Lake Plantation. In 1927, he was again involved in relief work, supervising relief operations during extensive floods in the Greenville area. It was reported that his gracious personality earned him the love and respect of people of all races.

He began writing poetry in 1911 and continued most of his life. In 1941, a year before he died, he published an autobiography, *Lanterns on the Levee, Recollections of a Planter's Son*. In August 1952, *The Reader's Digest* carried his life story in "The Most Unforgettable Character I've Met." Percy died in Greenville, on January 21, 1942.

This hymn was inspired by Mk. 1:16–20:

> As Jesus passed along the Sea of Galilee, he saw Simon and his brother Andrew casting a net into the sea—for they were fishermen. And Jesus said to them, "Follow me and I will make you fish for people." And immediately they left their nets and followed him. As he went a little farther, he saw James son of Zebedee and his brother John, who were in their boat mending the nets. Immediately he called them; and they left their father Zebedee in the boat with the hired men, and followed him.

The hymn text appeared first in Percy's volume of collected poems, *Enzio's Kingdom, and Other Poems*, 1924, under the heading of "His Peace," and originally began, "I love to think of them at dawn / Beneath the frail pink sky. / Casting their nets in Galilee / And fish-hawks circling by / Casting their nets in Galilee, / Just off the hills of brown." The text came under some criticism in the review process for *The Hymnal 1982* due to stanza three, where Percy implies that the Fourth Gospel and the Book of Revelation were written by the same person, but poetry prevailed over historicity.

The tune, written for *The Hymnal 1940*, undergirds the text with a strong melodic outline and measures of unequal length.

"The peace of God, it is no peace, / but strife closed in the sod. / Yet let us pray for but one thing— / the marvelous peace of God."

Ever since the first fishermen cast aside their nets and followed the strangely compelling itinerant preacher, Christians have found that their faith has led them into places they would not have chosen to go. What kind of peace is the peace of God that fills our hearts "brimful, and breaks them too"?

The peace of God is surely not the "opiate of the people," despite the opinion of Karl Marx. Rather, the peace of God is the quality of being so centered on eternal truth that it becomes possible for us to move out into the world around us in ways we might never expect.

Does that mean we ought not to seek comfort and stability through our faith in God? Of course we may—in fact it is the prerequisite for movement in both the spiritual and physical spheres.

I have been studying physical movement for years through various dance and exercise techniques, including hatha yoga and t'ai chi. Every technique, when properly taught, emphasizes that efficient movement springs from our body's center. Strong abdominal muscles help us stand in correct alignment and give us power to move our limbs. Noticing where our weight enters the floor when we are standing, walking, or dancing makes it possible to move in both simple and intricate ways without injury. We are never told simply to copy the movements of the instructor, but to become so familiar with the movements that they become natural for our bodies.

Certainly the same is true for our movement in faith. First, we must know where we are: centered in God. We must know God with our whole being, not merely intellectually or vicariously. That kind of knowledge provides a stability that gives us comfort.

Through building that comfort and strength within ourselves, we are able to go beyond ourselves, just as the strength of the dancer's deepest muscles makes it possible to fly through the air in a *tour jeté*. Centered in the Jesus Christ who called Peter and Andrew, James and John, we also can listen to Jesus' call, and have the strength to follow him wherever he leads us.

Hymn 665

All my hope on God is founded

Robert Seymour Bridges (1844–1930), alt., after Joachim Neander (1650–1680)

Joachim Neander was the foremost hymn writer of the German Reformed Church, the "Paul Gerhardt of the Calvinists." After a boisterous student life typical of seventeenth-century Germany, Neander served as a tutor in Frankfort and Heidelberg. He was introduced to Pietism, and became acquainted with the movement's leader, Philip Spener. Neander became headmaster of the grammar school at Düsseldorf, and five years later went to serve as an unordained assistant in a church in Bremen. However, because of his zealous religious practices and preaching, he was frequently in trouble with the church authorities. He sought release in communion with nature, in prayer, and in composing hymns. His great love of nature often led him to the valley of Düssel, ultimately named after him as the "Neanderthal" (Neander Valley), where it is said that he wrote many of his hymns. (It was here in 1856 that the skeleton of *Homo neanderthalensis* was discovered.) Neander died of tuberculosis at the age of thirty, having already produced sixty hymns.

Robert Bridges, the son of a wealthy squire, was educated at Eton and Corpus Christi College, Oxford, after which he studied medicine at St. Bartholomew's Hospital. His plan was to practice medicine until the age of forty and then devote himself to poetry, but he had to give up his practice because of ill health a few years before his planned retirement. He then moved to the Berkshire village of Yattendon where he lived and wrote for the next thirty years. A prolific writer, he was a friend of Gerard Manley Hopkins, whose complete poems Bridges eventually published.

His work with the village choir led him to an interest in hymnody and to the publication of the landmark collection, the *Yattendon Hymnal*, considered "easily the most distinguished of individual contributions to modern hymnology." Forty-four of the hymns in the *Yattendon Hymnal* were translations or adaptations by Bridges himself. Erik Routley writes that Bridges "did more than any other person to raise English hymnody to the level of respectable literature, redeeming it from both the crudity of the 18th c. and the conventionality of the 19th."

Bridges was named poet laureate in 1913; he continued writing until 1929, when his magnum opus, the *Testament of Beauty*, was published.

"All my hope on God is founded" was said by Bridges to be "a free version of a hymn by Joachim Neander." He did not really translate his German originals, but used them merely as a suggestion, sometimes adding new verses of his own. Percy Dearmer pointed out that, "although the individualistic note of the post-Luther German pietism is here retained in the opening stanzas, the hymn is on the whole on a wider and more modern note, and in line with [Bridge's] final mature thought in the *Testament of Beauty*."[69]

The tune was written by the composer Herbert Howells, who recalled that, upon receiving a request for a hymn tune, he wrote it in its entirety while still at the breakfast table where he had been opening the mail. The tune honors the composer's son Michael, who died in childhood.

"All my hope on God is founded." But how do we know we can depend on that hope? Does God truly wish to shower us with blessings? This hymn suggests a joyous answer: that one of the ways we know we can depend on God is through the beauty that surrounds us.

I suspect that the reason Joachim Neander found the solace of God during his walks in the verdant valley of Düssel, and Robert Bridges found comfort during an illness which cut short the course of his medical career, was their jubilant certainty that God desired them to share their Creator's joy. Bridges was later to write of "Beauty, the eternal Spouse of the Wisdom of God and Angel of his Presence thru' all creation, fashioning her new love-realm in the mind of man."[70]

Beauty is one of God's "lures" in winning us over: "pleasure leads us where we go." I remember a self-proclaimed atheist who finally made his way into my meditation class at Trinity Church after months of attending the weekday concert series. As he listened to great music in that holy space, he had begun to consider, for the first time, that there might be a reality behind the events of everyday life. He now calls himself an agnostic, and God is not done with him yet. He continues to explore the mystery behind music's power to move and enchant him.

Even the very young can perceive the sacred through their encounters with beauty. In a pre-school class in which I used the arts in Christian education, I brought in a collection of old Christmas cards which depicted the Annunciation of the Angel Gabriel to Mary, and let the children pick their favorites. One energetic little boy zeroed in on a Renaissance painting, his eyes alight—"I've got to have this!"—and clasped it to his heart.

For people like this little boy, God shines through such a painting; for others, music is God's voice. For others, it is poetry, or dance, or the loveliness of nature. It is the jubilation of our souls in response to these things that causes them to be channels of the divine. And when they become such channels, they convey the mystery of the Creator, the love of the Son, and the energy of the Spirit, better than any theological treatise.

When we are in despair, we ache for God's solace. But God calls to us also through our moments of pure delight. They reassure us that we can found our hope on a God who loves us.

The gift of beauty is a healing gift; through it, God's creativity constantly strengthens and renews us as human beings. In fashioning things of beauty ourselves, we share something of what it means to be made in the image of God.

As beings made in God's image, we become more fully human when we allow ourselves to find pleasure in the exquisiteness with which God has surrounded us. After all, God's greatest gift, Jesus Christ, was not only Goodness, Wisdom, and Truth personified: he was also a human being, able to take pleasure in good wine at a wedding feast. God wants us to enjoy the bounteous gifts we are daily given. And that is a God on whom I am willing to found all my hope!

Hymn 680

O God, our help in ages past

Isaac Watts (1674–1748)

Isaac Watts, the son of a nonconformist church deacon, was raised on the Psalms. The story is told that, when his father was imprisoned for his religious views, his mother carried young Isaac in her arms to the prison gate, where she on the outside and he on the inside sang together metrical versions of the Psalms. Later Isaac was to criticize these translations and accept the challenge to write better ones. Instead of being content with a metric translation of the original Hebrew, he set for himself the task of Christianizing the psalm. In making it reflect contemporary thoughts and feelings, he became the creator of the modern English hymn. During his lifetime, he produced about six hundred hymns, a book of *Logic*, and four major theological works.

"O God, our help in ages past," a paraphrase of Psalm 90, can be found in practically every English language hymnal in the world. It was written around the year 1714, when Queen Anne was near death and there was widespread anxiety about her successor. Many people feared that England would soon be torn by civil strife.

The hymn, originally containing nine stanzas, was published in Watts's The *Psalms of David* in 1719.

It is considered to be one of finest texts in English hymn literature, and was sung at Sir Winston Churchill's funeral on January 30, 1965, in St. Paul's Cathedral, London.

Handel used the tune, by William Croft, in an anthem entitled "O Praise the Lord" and Bach used it in his great Fugue in E-flat Major, often called the "St. Anne Fugue"; its matching with Watts's text did not occur until early in the nineteenth century.

Our era is an exciting one. We are on the move! We are able to see more of the world than at any time in history. Modern transportation can whisk us across an ocean or a continent in a few hours. We can choose to leave one job in order to work in a more challenging or more lucrative one many miles away. We put our home on the market, and go house-hunting in a distant city. People seldom spend all their lives in one place.

I did live in one place for my first twenty-three years, with the exception of my years at college. As a child, I was so fond of my home that I couldn't imagine ever moving. I remember weeping when, one night after I had been tucked into bed, I overheard my parents discuss "moving to Connecticut." (We didn't.) When I was in third grade and went away with a classmate for a week at her family's beach cottage, the ache to return home finally became so acute that, by the time I was deposited at my door, I had dissolved into tears. After my father died and my mother decided to move to an apartment, I could not believe she was selling my childhood home, although by that time my husband and I had our own. History repeated itself many years later, when we decided to sell our children's childhood home, and the youngest, who had returned to the nest after graduate school, felt similarly uprooted. As I remember, he said, "You could at least wait until I could afford to buy it."

Whether we live for many years in one place, or lead a more transient life-style, a home remains both a necessity and a symbol. Our home is our shelter, our protection, a place of comfort where we can be ourselves. It is painful when our homes are places of discord or abuse, and it is even more of a tragedy should we be one of the too many men, women, and children who have no home at all.

For along with the thirst for change and new experiences lies a universal hunger for stability. And that is probably the reason most of us love our homes.

Our homes may be symbols of that stability, but they do not suffice in the long run. They themselves are transitory, subject to the whims of weather and aging. Their roofs and walls may have sheltered the lives of our families, but they are no more permanent than our own bodies. I hear the reminder in the haunting "Here on earth have we no continuing place" in the Brahms *Requiem*, and I read the reminder in the news and the obituaries of every newspaper I open.

Earthly life is impermanent. If we depend on it for stability, we will be spiritually homeless.

Where is stability? "Lord, you have been our refuge, from one generation to another. Before the mountains were brought forth, or the land and the earth were born, from age to age you are God." Our stability, "while life shall last" and also beyond death, is God, our eternal home.

Hymn 687, 688

A mighty fortress is our God

Martin Luther (1483–1546); tr. Frederic Henry Hedge (1805–1890)

The hymnologist Erik Routley writes that "the success of any movement in culture or religion requires at least two people: the one who thought of it and the one who made it stick."[71] Although the Reformation had been brewing for at least 150 years before Martin Luther, it was Luther's peculiar genius to "make the Reformation stick." Many of his reforms stemmed from the belief that all Christians should be treated by the church as adult participants in worship. Luther accomplished much of this through the power of language. He wrote a German Catechism and translated a Bible that is the foundation of the modern German language. In addition, out of his concern for the people's participation in the liturgy, Luther created a uniquely German hymnody: "It is my intention to make German psalms for the people, spiritual songs whereby the word of God may be kept alive in them by singing."[72]

Eine Feste Burg ("A mighty fortress is our God") ranks among the most important of all

Christian hymns. It is one of the earliest examples of the genre of psalm paraphrase.

Its text was called by the poet Heine "the *Marseillaise* of the Reformation";[73] others called it "God Almighty's Grenadier March" or "The Battle Hymn of the Reformation."[74] This view of the hymn's purpose was given musical reinforcement by such composers as Mendelssohn in his *Reformation Symphony*, Meyerbeer in his opera *Les Hugenotten*, and Wagner in his *Kaisersmarsch*.

This interpretation, however, runs counter to Luther's understanding of his own hymn, which he entitled "A Hymn of Comfort." He envisioned it as an expression of the reasons for Christian hope in times of trial and conflict, not as a vehicle of belligerent Protestantism.

Luther is known to have found comfort in Psalm 46, on which this hymn is based. He himself wrote a brief outline of the psalm, which parallels his hymnic form of the text:

> This is a psalm of thanksgiving which the people of Israel sang at that time in response to the miracles of God, who had defended and sustained the city of Jerusalem, where they lived, against the rantings and ravings of all kings and nations, and preserved it in

> peace against all war and conflict. Then, speaking after the manner of scripture, the essence of the city is portrayed as a little spring, a small rivulet, that will not run dry, in contrast to the great rivers and oceans of the nations (that is, the great kingdoms, principalities and estates) that will dry up and disappear.
>
> But we sing in praise to God because he is with us—God who miraculously preserves his Word and Christendom against the gates of hell, against the ravings of all devils, fanatical spirits, the world, the flesh, sin, death, etc., so that our little spring remains a living fountain, while foul and stinking drains, puddles and cisterns will run dry.[75]

Luther never drew a strong line of distinction between the hardships of life and the internal struggles of the soul. The hymn was written sometime around 1527–1528, and causes for anxiety were plentiful. In 1527, Wittenberg was experiencing an outbreak of the plague, and a report had been received that a man named Leonard Kaiser had been martyred for confessing the evangelical faith. It was the tenth anniversary of the posting of the *95 Theses*, and Luther's wife was pregnant with their second child.

Luther interprets Psalm 46 in strongly Christological terms, anticipating Isaac Watts by almost two centuries. He pictures the strife between life and death as the struggle between Christ and the devil. Robin Leaver writes that the key to the whole hymn may be found in the final line of the final stanza: "his kingdom is for ever."[76] Toward the end of 1528, Luther was also working on his catechetical exposition of the Lord's Prayer, and he wrote the following about "Thy kingdom come":

> What is the kingdom of God? Answer: Simply what we learned in the Creed, namely, that God sent his Son, Christ our Lord, into the world to redeem and deliver us from the power of the devil and to bring us to himself and rule as a king of righteousness, life, and salvation against sin, death, and an evil conscience. . . . So we pray that, led by the Holy Spirit, many may come into the kingdom of grace and become partakers of salvation, so that we may all remain together eternally in this kingdom which has now made its appearance among us.[77]

Within Luther's own lifetime, *Ein feste Burg* was translated into many European languages, including one by Miles Coverdale in his *Goostly psalmes and spirituall songes* in 1535. Almost five centuries later, the hymn is sung in at least two hundred different languages, and there are about one hundred different English translations, each one an attempt at the difficult task of presenting Luther's rugged poetry in the form of English verse.

The translation by Frederick H. Hedge, a Unitarian minister, which first appeared in 1852, is the one used predominantly in North American hymnals. Born in Cambridge, Massachusetts, Hedge was sent to study in Germany when he was thirteen years old, graduated from Harvard, studied theology, and was ordained in 1829. A pastor closely associated with the Transcendental Movement, he was also professor of both ecclesiastical history and of German at Harvard University.

The text is matched with two versions of Luther's tune: Luther's rhythmic form of the tune, and its later, more familiar form harmonized by Johann Sebastian Bach.

I had never been inside a fortress like the ones Luther knew until we visited Salzburg a few years ago as part of a musical pilgrimage entitled "Tracing Mozart." Our quest took us on a funicular railway up the Mönchsberg, a hill overlooking the old town, to the Hohensalzburg, or "Salzburg castle," where we were to attend a concert. I had visited American colonial forts and Norman castles, but I have never seen such a fortification as this one. As we disembarked and walked the path to the entrance, high above us rose wall piled upon wall, all many feet thick. The mighty medieval and baroque edifice must have been, in its day, truly impervious to attack.

I think that the fondness for such enclosures is not merely a response to danger from outside, but the result of an innate sense of the comfort we feel when we find a safe space we call our own. I remember the delight of crawling into the snow fort my brothers and I built by our front door, the delicious world of the card table covered over with a bedsheet, the secret place under the forsythia bush in our back yard. These were places no adult body could enter; they were the fortifications of childhood.

The Hohensalzburg and its kindred enclosures, like our childhood secret places, keep out the rest of the world. Perhaps the closest equivalent today is the gated community, where those who can afford it can be protected from the dangers, real or imagined, lurking outside.

For Luther, God's presence was strength, solid as the walls of Salzburg's castle. He had experience of the presence of evil: the world, "with devils filled," threatened to undo him. Protection from the outside, in the manner of a castle or card table, would not suffice against "the prince of darkness grim." Instead, the fortress needed to be within: the presence of Christ Jesus in his soul. Its weight grounded him in God's grace, its permanence reminded him of God's everlastingness.

Luther's fortress did not keep out the rest of the world. Instead, it protected him from the enemy within his own soul whose weapons were despair, cynicism, hatred, and fear. Because of the strength of his belief in God's grace, he had the courage to live and to write as God had called him to do. God's grace enabled him to remind others of God's presence and protection in their lives. This grace, stronger than any earthly castle, gives us the will to battle, on behalf of our world, against all that is not of God.

Hymn 690

Guide me, O thou great Jehovah

William Williams (1717–1791); tr. Peter Williams (1722–1796)

William Williams, known as the "Sweet Singer of Wales," was born at Cefn-y-Coed, in the parish of Llanfair-y-bryn near Llandovery. He was the son of a prosperous Welsh farmer and received a good education. He originally studied medicine, but decided to enter the ministry after hearing Howell Harris, the great leader of the Welsh Methodist Revival, preach at Talgarth. He was ordained a deacon in Church of England in 1740. Because of his Methodist leanings and his refusal to confine his preaching to his own parish, he was denied ordination as a priest. He then left the parish and became an itinerant evangelist. For over fifty years, he was to travel an average of nearly three thousand miles a year throughout Wales, often with his wife, a singer.

Williams's hymns were his chief contribution to religious life and literature in Wales. He wrote more than eight hundred in Welsh and another one hundred in English.

"Guide me, O thou great Jehovah," originally in Welsh, was translated by Peter Williams in 1771. The author accepted part of it, added a stanza, and printed it on a leaflet captioned, "A Favorite Hymn sung by Lady Huntingdon's Young Collegians Printed by the desire of many Christian friends. Lord, give it thy blessing!"[78] It was later printed in Williams's collection of hymns, *Caniadau y rhai sydd ar y Mor o Wydr (The Songs of Those upon the Sea of Glass).*

Elvit Lewis said of him, "What Paul Gerhardt has been to Germany, what Isaac Watts has been to England, that and more has William Williams been to the little Principality of Wales."[79]

The tune, by Williams's compatriot John Hughes, has long been popular at Welsh hymn festivals and is still sung fervently, with this text, at football matches in Wales.

Many of us have romantic ideas of what a pilgrimage entails, but William Williams knew the truth. In his near-half-century of travels the length and breadth of Wales, he must have often prayed, "Guide me, O thou great Jehovah, / pilgrim through this barren land."

During one of the summers in which my husband and I guided a group journey to England, we stayed in the town of Ashford, close to the Pilgrims' Way, a route used by medieval travelers between Winchester and Canterbury. On a free day, some of our number decided to walk part of that historic footpath. Since others of the group chose to travel by coach to Canterbury later in the morning, the walkers planned to meet the coach at noon and travel the rest of the way with us. They studied the map carefully, and decided that they could easily travel the six miles to a crossroads marked "Godmersham" during the course of the morning.

At noon, the coach arrived at Godmersham and drew up alongside a stucco house with a pink rambler rose twining around its entrance. The sign said "Old Post Office," but it was obviously no longer in business; there was not a soul in sight. We sat waiting for nearly half an hour, but finally had to leave a message with a man tending his garden down the lane and drive off towards Canterbury without our pilgrims.

When the coach returned to pick up the wanderers an hour later, they had finally arrived at the Godmersham. It turned out that, though the footpath was a mere six miles, it was not by any means horizontal. The modern-day pilgrims had needed to walk uphill and downhill, climb over fences and styles, and pick their way carefully through pastures dotted with cow pats. It had not been a leisurely walk, but a strenuous effort.

Like the Pilgrims' Way, our earthly pilgrimage is usually anything but a straight and level path. Instead, the landscape often challenges us; the walk from birth to death requires effort on our part.

William Williams knew that we do not walk alone. Sometimes the path is barren; we feel bored and listless, and it is difficult to summon the energy to put one foot in front of the other. At times like that, God is there as the bread of heaven, the traveler's sustenance. Sometimes our thirst—for love, for companionship, for consolation—almost overwhelms us. Then God provides living water, healing and surrounding us with compassion. Sometimes we feel we are lost, yet the God who led the Israelites with fire by night and a cloud by day will not abandon us. Should we become fearful about "treading the verge of Jordan" as we face our deaths, the Jehovah whose power led Jesus through the darkness of the grave into everlasting life will walk beside us then, as well.

Hymn 693

Just as I am, without one plea
Charlotte Elliott (1789–1871)

Some of the most popular hymns of the Victorian era were "invalid hymns," and many of these were written by Charlotte Elliott. Elliott was born in Clapham, England. She began at an early age to write humorous poems, and was interested in music and painting. At the age of thirty-two, she suffered an illness which resulted in her becoming a permanent invalid. The next year, she met César Malan, an evangelist from Geneva, who inspired her to devote the rest of her life to religious and humanitarian pursuits. Her correspondence with him lasted forty years.

In 1834 she undertook to edit the *Christian Remembrancer Pocketbook*, and prepared this volume annually for twenty-five years. She assisted in the publication of *The Invalid's Hymn Book*, printed in Dublin in 1836. Her hymns appear in that collection, as well as in many others: *Hours of Sorrow Cheered and Comforted* (1836); *Hymns for a Week* (1839); *Thoughts in Verse on Sacred Subjects* (1869); and her brother's collection *Psalms and Hymns for Public, Private, and Social Worship* (1838–1848).

This hymn first appeared in Elliott's *Invalid's Hymn Book* with the heading, "Him that cometh unto Me, I will in no wise cast out" (Jn.6:37). It was written at Westfield Lodge, Brighton, where her brother, the Rev. Henry V. Elliott, had arranged a bazaar to raise funds for building a college, to be named St. Margaret's Hall. Because she was neither able to attend or to help in any way, Elliott, oppressed by feelings of uselessness, finally penned the poem in order to overcome her sense of futility. The irony of the story is that the sale of this hymn aided the cause more than any bazaar: the title page of the various editions of *Hymns for a Week*, in which it was later published, contain the note, "Sold for the benefit of St. Margaret's Hall, Brighton."

The hymn was a great favorite of William Wordsworth's daughter, Dora, whose widower sent a message to Elliott in July of 1847 to thank her for her beautiful hymn. It had been of great comfort to his wife while she lay on her death bed: "I do not think Mr. Wordsworth could bear to have it repeated in his presence, but he is not the less sensible of the solace it gave his one and matchless daughter."[80]

A similar tribute was given by Elliott's brother, who wrote, "In the course of a long ministry, I hope I have been permitted to see some fruit of my labors; but I feel far more has been done by a single hymn of my sister's."[81] After her death, more than a thousand letters were found among her belongings thanking her for the hymn.

The text is matched with the tune with which it has been popularly associated in the United States since 1860.

I used to smile at what I considered to be the sentimentality of this hymn text until I read the story of Charlotte Elliott. An invalid who ministered to others through her poetry, she obviously met a real need in an era before awareness of preventive health care and the miracles of modern medicine were the norm. Her *Hours of Sorrow Cheered and Comforted* contained titles such as: "On a restless night in illness," "To one whose mind was disordered by grief," "To a mother, on the death of a child of great promise," and "To one deprived of hearing at church through deafness." Because she herself had studied in the school of suffering, she could teach others. She spoke to people who felt useless or stricken, and her words rang true.

It is only to healthy people in the prime of life in the twenty-first century that these words are likely to sound sentimental. There are many others who have learned, through hard experience, the wisdom of Elliott's words.

I frequently visit a local extended care retirement community where there is a nursing wing. Residents of the independent living units who are ill or have undergone surgery may stay in the nursing wing for a time until they have strength to manage life on their own. But there are some permanent residents of the nursing wing who could tell us a great deal about uselessness.

Some of them could have written a poem similar to Elliott's. There is a beautiful woman who owned a fashionable dress shop on the East Coast until a stroke deprived her of speech. No longer an efficient and successful businesswoman, she is nevertheless a smiling presence in the retirement center, cheering others by her wonderful outfits and flamboyant earrings and her obvious zest for life.

Her neighbor is a widow with what is called "brittle" diabetes, and her insulin level must be monitored day and night. We had looked at the gracious and hospitable house she had lived in when we were seeking a place to live in Oberlin, and I was drawn to her warmth and friendliness. These qualities have not diminished since she became a resident in the nursing wing; she herself embodies the hospitality I recognized in her former home.

There is a young man named Jeff who is afflicted with Lou Gehrig's Disease, or Amyotrophic Lateral Sclerosis, a progressive degeneration of the nerve cells in the brain and spinal cord that control the voluntary muscles. The illness, mercifully, does not at this point affect his mind, but Jeff cannot move and he spends his waking hours in a wheelchair. His call button for the nursing station is a mouth-operated device. He cannot feed himself, but depends on the resident assistants and the good will of volunteers from the retirement community.

When I asked Jeff how he was the other day, he said, "I'm fine; I'm just 'Jeffing.'" He could have said, "Just as I am without one plea." Jeff has learned a new approach to life, in which the value of thoughtful, reflective being supersedes the usual societal value given to usefulness. Because he is so good at "Jeffing," Jeff has many visitors: professors, students, retirement community residents, people from the town, and myself. Going to see Jeff is like visiting a guru, who reminds us of why we are called human beings, rather than human doings.

I would like to think that we can all learn the value of "Jeffing" or "Nancying" or "Whatever-your-name-is-ing" without being struck by illness or accident or extreme old age. Our whole lives long, we need to remind ourselves that we are valuable in God's eyes, not because we are capable, but because we are ourselves.

I am sure that none of us arrives at that insight easily. It is human nature to resist dependence and weakness with all our power: very likely we would be "tossed about / with many a conflict, many a doubt," should we ourselves end up in a wheelchair. Elliott's poem reassures us that, on the other side of that struggle, lies a treasure: the absolute dependence, not merely on others, but on the fact that God's great love, with all its breadth, length, depth, and height, is ours, just as we are.

Hymn 699

Jesus, Lover of my soul

Charles Wesley (1707–1788)

Charles Wesley was the eighteenth of nineteen children of an Anglican clergyman and his wife. He was educated at Westminster School and at Christ Church, Oxford, where he founded a group nicknamed the "Holy Club" or "Methodists" because of its members' devotion to Bible study, prayer, frequent Communion, and the visitation of prisoners and the sick. Ordained in 1735, Charles sailed the next month to Georgia with his brother John to serve as General Oglethorpe's secretary in the new colony. On board ship they became acquainted with twenty-six Moravians who were also passengers. In his journal on January 25, 1736, John described what happened during one of their meetings on board:

> In the midst of the psalm wherewith their service began, the sea broke over, split the mainsail in pieces, covered the ship and poured in between the decks, as if the great deep had already swallowed us up. A terrible screaming began among the English. The Germans looked up, and without intermis sion sang on. I asked one of them afterwards, "Was you not afraid?" He answered, "Thank God, no."[82]

This event obviously left a lasting impression. Returning to England after half a year, Charles' ship encountered another frightening storm, and when they finally reached land, on December 3, 1736, Wesley wrote in his journal, "I knelt down and blessed the Hand that had conducted me through such inextricable mazes." Soon the brothers fell in with the Moravians once again, and on Whitsunday 1738, Charles had an evangelical conversion. A few days later his brother John experienced a similar conversion, recorded in his journal:

> In the evening I went very unwillingly to a society [a meeting of Moravians] in Aldersgate Street, where one was reading Luther's *Preface to the Epistle to the Romans*. About a quarter before nine, while he was describing the change which God works in the heart through faith in Christ, I felt my heart strangely warmed. I felt that I did trust in Christ, Christ alone for salvation; and an assurance was given to me that he had taken away my sins, even mine, and saved me from the jaws of sin and death.[83]

Charles joined his brother John in itinerant preaching, and the brothers—who never left the Church of England—figure jointly in the calendar of the Book of Common Prayer (1979), commemorated together as "priests, poets, and teachers of the faith."

Of all the 6,500 hymns Charles Wesley wrote, this is generally considered to be his finest. Henry

Ward Beecher, noted American preacher of the past century, once wrote,

> I would rather have written that hymn of Wesley's than to have the fame of all the kings hat ever sat on earth; it is more glorious, it has more power in it. I would rather be the author of that hymn than to hold the wealth of the richest man in New York. He will die after a little while, pass out of men's thought, what will there be to speak of him? But people will go on singing that hymn until the last trump brings forth the angel band; and then I think it will mount upon some lips to the very pres ence of God.[84]

The hymn is matched with a strong Welsh tune, common to English-language hymnals around the world.

When I sing this hymn, with its melody like the great roll of the waves, I like to think of Charles Wesley on board ship during the storm described in his brother's journal.

There is something about being in a storm at sea that makes us recognize our helplessness. On land, we can take shelter; but there is no shelter in the primordial vastness of the deep. We are at the mercy of the fierce wind and the rolling waves, hoping that our craft is worthy and our captain skilled.

The ocean is a thing of beauty and also of terror. No wonder that people are perennially fascinated by tales of ocean voyages, from *The Odyssey* and *Moby Dick* to the sinking of the *Titanic*. I sailed to Europe once on a small student ship and remember standing on deck, looking at water extending to the horizon as far as the eye could see. Air travel has erased that experience of the ocean's vastness for most of us, but, should we have a window seat, we can sometimes see the deep waters below, reminding us.

No wonder that the unpredictability of storms at sea has become a favorite metaphor for the times when we feel buffeted and battered by life's events. When Charles Wesley faced dangerously hostile crowds during his itinerant preaching, he very likely compared those situations to his eventful sea voyage with the Moravians.

Who is our refuge in life's storms? Where is our harbor? Our haven is the heaven of Jesus' presence. It is difficult to miss the common derivation of those very similar words.

The image of water is transformed in the course of the hymn. The angry waters of the ocean are replaced by the healing waters of streams and the fountain of life. These friendlier waters represent God's grace.

But I like to think of the image of the ocean as capable of transformation, too. Perhaps the ocean can remind us that, rather than always seeking refuge from the storms of life, we can find God in them. God need not be just a healing stream or a gentle fountain. God can be the ocean, too.

The ocean of God is vast and uncharted territory. But we do know some things about the way God acts in the world.

There are wonders in the depths of the ocean that are accessible only to the deep-sea diver's—or the saint's or the mystic's—eye. Not being deep-sea divers, we often look only on the turbulent surface of events when they trouble us, but do not realize that fathoms below that surface is another world, unseen.

And our gaze is so limited! We can't even imagine what lies beyond the sea's wide horizons. The ocean is the domain of the unknown and of mystery.

And yet it is there, supporting us. When I swim in the surf, I have learned that, if I permit it, the sea carries me. Sometimes I float on a calm sea. Sometimes the waves are strong, and they can be frightening. But I have learned not to fight them. They will continue to carry me if I do not struggle.

Jesus walked on the waves towards a small boat in the Sea of Galilee to comfort his frightened disciples caught in a storm. The sea supported him. And the sea that is God will carry us, too, and we will discover, perhaps, that we will need to find no other refuge or haven, but can just rest in that truth.

Hymn 707

Take my life, and let it be

Frances Ridley Havergal (1836–1879)

Frances Ridley Havergal was born in Astley, England. Delicate health forced her to restrict her activities as a child, but her accomplishments were numerous and varied. At the age of seven, she began to write verses, and her poems soon appeared in *Good Words* and other religious journals. She eventually mastered several modern languages as well as Hebrew. She also composed music; it is interesting to note that Havergal had a life-long correspondence with Fanny Crosby, the blind American writer of gospel music.

Following an intense religious experience as a young girl, of which she later wrote that "earth and heaven seemed brighter from that moment," she gave herself unstintingly to helping others, so far as her strength allowed. She was much sought after for her counsel, which often drained her but which she gave without reservation. On one occasion, she expressed the hope that "the angels would have orders to let her alone a bit when she first got to heaven." It was said of her that she "disclosed a remarkable Christian character, exhibiting all the beauty, freshness and charm of that life of complete and happy consecration which was the chief subject of her song."[85]

Many of Havergal's hymns were printed in leaflets, which were then transferred to several volumes. After her death, her sister collected them into the volume *Poetical Works*, published in 1884.

The text of "Take my life, and let it be" was written while Havergal was visiting Areley House in Worcestershire. She later wrote:

> Perhaps you will be interested to know the origin of the consecration hymn "Take My

> Life." I went for a little visit of five days. There were ten persons in the house, some unconverted and long-prayed-for, some converted but not rejoicing Christians. He gave me the prayer, "Lord, give me all in this house!" And He just did. Before I left the house, everyone had got a blessing! The last night of my visit I was too happy to sleep, and passed most of the night in praise and renewal of my own consecration, and these little couplets formed themselves and chimed in my heart one after another till they finished with "Ever, only, *all* for Thee."[86]

The hymn was first published in *Songs of Grace and Glory* (1874). It has been translated into many European, African, and Asian languages. Havergal later wrote a book, *Kept for the Master's Work*, based on the hymn.

The text is matched with a tune written by the precentor of Durham Cathedral, John Bacchus Dykes, around 1860.

What can we give to God and to others when we feel we are utterly useless? Frances Ridley

Havergal knew the answer to that question: We can give ourselves.

When I work with the aged and infirm in nursing homes, it is quite apparent that the frequent depression I observe is the result of the residents' feeling of uselessness. Men who once knew upward mobility, power, and prestige are confined to wheelchairs. Women who raised families now must be fed and bathed by others.

I have always thought that the patron saint of the physically weak could be Julian of Norwich. She did not have confinement forced upon her, like my elderly friends in the nursing home. Rather, she chose to live her life in one small room called an "anchorhold" beside the Church of St. Julian in Norwich, where she spent a life of prayer. There were many like her in fourteenth-century Norwich, but we know Julian best because she has left us her spiritual diary, *Revelations of Divine Love*.

What Julian gave to the people of Norwich was her presence. She was a praying presence, first of all, like a spiritual powerhouse attached to the church. And she was a listening presence. People came to the window of her small cell and told her their troubles. It was a difficult time, full of civil unrest and the ominous shadow of the plague. Julian counseled the troubled and consoled the sorrowful. She was a beacon of God's love in a dark era.

My guess is that such was the kind of presence that Frances Havergal brought to her friends and acquaintances. Her usefulness lay not in what she could do, but in what she conveyed—not necessarily through her words but through her character. Her life, like Julian's, was a consecrated life. She gave her moments and her days to God. She offered her hands and her heart, her voice and powers of communication, her intellect and powers of thought, even her will and her decisions, to her Lord.

By modern standards, these two women's lives might not be seen as useful. But our blindness is a symptom of society's devaluation of the elderly or the disabled. And it also prevents those of us who are young and active from preparing for the time in our own lives when we will no longer be "useful" in the world's eyes. Despite the concern about financial planning for retirement, there is little guidance concerning spiritual planning for the last years of life.

We can begin right now preparing for that time by remembering that who we are is more important than what we do, and by praying, with Frances and with Julian, "Take my life, and let it be consecrated, Lord, to thee."

Notes

1. Hugh Johnson, *The Principles of Gardening* (London: Mitchell Beazley Publishers Ltd., 1979), 86.
2. David Austin, David Austin's *English Roses* (London: Conran Octopus Ltd., 1993), 11.
3. Susan S. Tamke, *Make a Joyful Noise* (Columbus, OH: Ohio University Press, 1978), 85.
4. Raymond F. Glover, ed., *The Hymnal 1982 Companion, Vol. Three A* (New York: The Church Hymnal Corporation, 1994), 200.
5. Tamke, 84.
6. Wesley Milgate, *Songs of the People of God* (London, 1982), 293.
7. P. Dearmer, ed. *Songs of Praise Discussed* (London,1933), 90–91.
8. Lionel Adey, *Hymns and the Christian "Myth"* (Vancouver: University of British Columbia Press, 1986), 167.
9. Glover, ed., *The Hymnal 1982 Companion, Volume Three A*, 156.
10. Ibid.
11. Samuel Willoughby Duffield, *English Hymns: Their Authors and History* (New York: Funk & Wagnalls Company, 1856), 272.
12. Pierre Teilhard de Chardin, *The Divine Milieu* (New York: Harper & Row, 1960), 110.
13. Glover, ed., *The Hymnal 1982 Companion, Vol. Three A*, 417.
14. Ruth Ellis Messenger, *Latin Hymns of the Middle Ages* (New York: Hymn Society of America, 1948), quoted in Mary Kay Stulken, *Hymnal Companion to the Lutheran Book of Worship* (Philadelphia Fortresss Press, 1981), 237.
15. W. Osbeck, *101 More Hymn Stories* (Grand Rapids, MI: Kregel Publications, 1985), 90.
16. Ibid., 91.
17. Quoted in *A Sourcebook about Christian Death* (Chicago: Liturgy Training Publications, 1990), 3.
18. LindaJo H. McKim, ed. *The Presbyterian Hymnal Companion* (Louisville, KY: Westminster/John Knox Press, 1993), 278.
19. John Julian, *A Dictionary of Hymnology, Vol.1* (New York: Dover Publications, Inc., 1957), 386.
20. Quoted in Albert C. Ronander and Ethel K. Porter, ed., *Guide to the Pilgrim Hymnal* (Philadelphia, Boston: United Church Press), 1966, 3.
21. McKim, 17.
22. Albert Edward Bailey, *The Gospel in Hymns*,

21. McKim, 17.
22. Albert Edward Bailey, *The Gospel in Hymns,* (New York: Charles Scribner's Sons, 1950), 144
23. Glover, ed., *The Hymnal Companion 1982, Volume Three A*, 117.
24. Percy Dearmer, *Songs of Praise Discussed* (London: Oxford University Press, 1933), 115.
25. Ibid.
26. Glover, ed. *The Hymnal 1982 Companion, Vol. Three A*, 362.
27. Erik Routley, *Hymns and the Faith* (Greenwich, CT: The Seabury Press, 1956), 71–72.
28. Ibid., 77–78.
29. Stulken, 273.
30. David Adam *The Edge of Glory: Prayers in the Celtic tradition* (Wilton, CT: 1988), 4.
31. Julian, 1149.
32. Thomas Cahill, *The Gifts of the Jews: How a Tribe of Desert Nomads Changed the Way Everyone Thinks and Feels* (New York: Nan A. Talese/Anchor Books, 1998).
33. Ibid., 63.
34. Ibid., 89.
36. Quoted in Ronander and Porter, 17.
37. Julian of Norwich, *Showings* (New York: Paulist Press, 1978), 279.
38. Thomas à Kempis, *The Imitation of Christ* (Mt. Vernon, NY: Peter Pauper Press), 10.
39. Ibid., 86.
40. Glover, ed. *The Hymnal 1982 Companion , Vol. Three B*, 866.
41. Ibid.
42. Murial Searle, John Ireland, *The Man and his Music* (Tunbridge Wells: Midas Books, 1979), quoted in McKim, 77.
43. A. M. Allchin and Esther de Waal, *Daily Readings from Prayers and Praises in the Celtic Tradition* (SpringWeld, IL: Templegate Publishers, 1986), 14.
44. For a further resource, see David Adam's book, *The Eye of the Eagle: Meditations on the hymn "Be thou my vision"* (London: Triangle, 1990).
45. Esther De Waal, *God under my Roof: Celtic Songs and Blessings* (Oxford: SLG Press, 1984), 9.

46. Ibid., 13–15.
47. Gracia Grindal, *The Hymn*, Vol.39, No. 2, 28.
48. Evelyn Underhill, *Practical Mysticism* (New York: E.P.Dutton & Co., Inc., 1960), 3.
49. John Julian, *A Dictionary of Hymnology, Volume II* (New York: Dover Publications, 1957), 1147.
50. Frederick Buechner, *Wishful Thinking: A Seeker's ABC* (New York: Harper & Row, 1973), 95.
51. Bailey, 54.
52. Ibid., 66.
53. Ibid., 67.
54. Ronander and Porter, 282.
55. Bailey, 38.
56. Ibid.
57. Ibid., 40.
58. John Bunyan, *The Pilgrim's Progress* (New York: The Century Co., 1898), 1.
59. *The Pilgrim's Progress*, 1684 edition.
60. Glover, ed. *The Hymnal 1982 Companion, Vol. Two*, 393.
61. Dearmer, 271.
62. Bunyan, vii.
63. John Dominic Crossan, *In Parables: The Challenge of the Historical Jesus* (New York: Harper & Row, 1973), xviii.
64. Louisa M. Alcott, *Little Women* (New York: Grosset & Dunlap, 1915), "Preface."
65. Buechner, 1–2.
66. Pseudo-Dionysius, "The Celestial Hierarchy,"*Pseudo-Dionysius: The Complete Works* (New York: Paulist Press, 1987), 154.
67. Glover, ed., *The Hymnal 1982 Companion, Vol. Two*, 325.
68. Glover, ed., *The Hymnal 1982 Companion, Vol. Three B*, 1185.
69. Ibid.,665.
70. From "A Testament of Beauty," quoted in Edward Thompson, *Robert Bridges* (London: Oxford University Press, 1944), 106.
71. Erik Routley, *Christian Hymns Observed* (Oxford: A. R. Mow-bray & Co.Ltd., 1983), 15.
72. Quoted in Winfred Douglas, *Church Music in History and Practice:*

Studies in the Praise of God (New York, Charles Scribner's Sons, 1937), 210–11.

73. Glover, ed., *The Hymnal 1982 Companion, Vol. Three B*, 1274.

74. Ibid., 1276.

75. *Martin Luthers Werke: Kirtische Gesamtausgabe* (Weimar, 1883–), Vol. 38, 35. Translation by Robin A. Leaver in Glover, ed., *The Hymnal 1982 Companion, Vol. Three B*, 1277.

76. Glover, ed., *The Hymnal 1982 Companion, Vol. Three B*, 1278.

77. T. G. Tappert, ed., *The Book of Concord: The Confessions of the Evangelical Lutheran Church*, (Philadelphia: Muhlenberg Press, 1959), 426–427.

78. McKim, 201.

79. Ronander and Porter, 76.

80. Glover, ed., *The Hymnal 1982 Companion, Vol. Three B*, 693.

81. J. Dahle, *Library of Christian Hymns* (Minneapolis, 1975), 642, quoted in Glover, *The Hymnal 1982 Companion, Vol. Three B*, 1297.

82. John Wesley, *The Journal of John Wesley* (London: Robert Culley, 1909), 142–143.

83. Ibid., 475–476.

84. Kenneth W. Osbeck, *101 Hymn Stories* (Grand Rapids, MI: Kregel Publications,1982), 130.

85. Ronander and Porter, 308.

86. McKim, 273.